100 FACTS

Leeds

First published in Great Britain in 2018
by Wymer Publishing
www.wymerpublishing.co.uk
Wymer Publishing is a trading name of Wymer (UK) Ltd

First edition. Copyright © 2018 Steve Horton / Wymer Publishing.

ISBN 978-1-908724-79-3

Edited by Jerry Bloom.

The Author hereby asserts his rights to be identified
as the author of this work in accordance with sections
77 to 78 of the Copyright, Designs & Patents Act 1988.

All rights reserved. No part of this publication may be
reproduced or transmitted in any form or by any means,
electronic or mechanical, including photocopying, or any
information storage and retrieval system, without written
permission from the publisher.

This publication is sold subject to the condition that it shall not,
by way of trade or otherwise, be lent, re-sold, hired out or
otherwise circulated without the publishers prior consent in any
form of binding or cover other than that in which it is published
and without a similar condition including this condition
being imposed on the subsequent purchaser.

Typeset by The Andys.
Printed and bound by Clays, Bungay, Suffolk

A catalogue record for this book is available from the British Library.

Cover design by The Andys.
Sketches by Becky Welton. © 2014.

10 FACTS

Leeds

Steve Horton

WYMER
PUBLISHING
Bedford, England

1904
LEEDS CITY

FACT 1

Prior to Leeds United their was a club called Leeds City who were formed following a meeting at the Griffin Hotel in Boar Lane in 1904.

Leeds City took over the Elland Road ground which was available after the demise of Holbeck rugby league club. After a season in the West Yorkshire League, they were elected to the Football League the following year and spent the next eleven years in the Second Division.

In 1912 Herbert Chapman, who would go on to have great success with Huddersfield and Arsenal, was appointed manager. He led the club to sixth and fourth place finishes but 1914-15 was disappointing when they slumped to fifteenth.

The Football League was then suspended due to the outbreak of World War One and competitions were run on regional lines. However when the Football League resumed for 1919-20, Leeds City were expelled after eight games when they were found guilty of financial irregularities. These included making illegal payments to players during the war.

Leeds City's players were then sold off in an auction which took place at the Metropole Hotel. The club's fixtures were taken over by Port Vale.

FACT 2

1919
LEEDS UNITED JOIN
THE MIDLAND LEAGUE

After Leeds City disbanded moves were quickly made to form a new club in the city.

On 17th October, the same day as the auction at the Metropole Hotel, Leeds United were formed after a meeting attended by 1,000 supporters.

Dick Ray, who had been a player with Leeds City between 1905 and 1908 was appointed team manager. The new club's first game on 15th November 1919 was a 5-2 defeat against Yorkshire Amateurs at Elland Road.

The following week Leeds United played their first competitive fixture, drawing 0-0 at home to Barnsley Reserves. This was in the Midland League, which they had been invited to join to take the place of Leeds City's reserves. Early results were disappointing however and United won only three of their first fifteen games.

In February 1920 new club owner Hilton Crowther brought in Arthur Fairclough as manager with Dick Ray as his assistant. Fairclough had won the FA Cup with Barnsley in 1912 and there was an improvement in the second half of the season, which ended in the club finishing twelfth out of eighteen teams.

FACT 3

1920 ELECTION TO THE FOOTBALL LEAGUE

After Leeds United were elected to Division Two of the Football League in 1920 they switched their colours to blue and white stripes, the same as Huddersfield.

Prior to taking over at United, Hilton Crowther had been Huddersfield's chairman and initially planned to amalgamate the two clubs and play at Elland Road. When opposition in Huddersfield scuppered those plans, he loaned United £35,000 to help build a club capable of challenging in the Football League.

After being elected to Division Two in May 1920, Fairclough set about putting together a side which was a mixture of talented young local players and experienced professionals. The kit was then changed from blue and gold to blue and white striped shirts with white shorts, just like Huddersfield.

The first game was ironically away to Port Vale, who had taken over Leeds City's fixtures the previous season. It ended in a 2-0 defeat for United, who then lost their first home league fixture 2-1 to South Shields. The third fixture however saw Port Vale beaten 3-1 at Elland Road.

United finished the season in a respectable fourteenth out of 22 teams. Crowds averaged 15,000 and there was every reason to be optimistic about the future.

1922
A HURRICANE FINISH

FACT 4

In a thrilling game against Coventry City in 1921-22, Leeds United scored three goals in the last ten minutes to seal victory.

United enjoyed an excellent start to the season and were top of Division Two at the end of

September, unbeaten in their first seven games. They couldn't keep this up though and by the time Coventry came to Elland Road on 25th March 1922 they were down to tenth.

In front of a crowd of 10,000 on a gloriously sunny day, the first half was rather dull but United took the lead after thirty minutes through Len Armitage. Twelve minutes into the second half Jack Swan doubled United's advantage but five minutes later Coventry pulled a goal back.

There was little else of incident until ten minutes from time when Swan made it 3-1, then soon afterwards Armitage got United's fourth. With a minute left Millard scored a consolation for Coventry from long range but there was still time for one more goal with Swan completing his hat-trick.

The *Yorkshire Post* headline read 'A Hurricane Finish' and it was the start of a six game winning run. They eventually finished in eighth position.

FACT 5

1924
DIVISION TWO
CHAMPIONS

In their fourth season in the Football League, Leeds United won the Division Two title.

United didn't get off to the best of starts, winning only one of their first six games. However seven straight wins took them to the top by the beginning of November.

In December United lost in successive weeks to promotion rivals Bury. This meant they dropped to second place but they returned to the top on Christmas Day with a 2-2 at Oldham. A 2-0 defeat at South Shields in the first fixture of 1924 saw United fall to third, but they then set off on another winning run, picking up maximum points from six successive games.

On 27th February United beat South Shields 2-1 at Elland Road to go back on top and they remained there for the rest of the season. The Yorkshire Post said that although cleverer teams had gone up 'no set of players has tried harder or trained more conscientiously'.

Promotion was secured with a 4-0 home win over Stockport County on 21st April in front of a crowd of 22,145. Five days later United beat Nelson 1-0 at Elland Road to wrap up the title and achieve Hilton Crowther's aim of Division One football.

FACT 6

1926
TOM JENNINGS' GOALS
KEEP UNITED UP

When Leeds avoided relegation in 1925-26 they were thankful for the goals of Tom Jennings.

United struggled for much of 1924-25 but the arrival of Jennings from Raith Rovers in March helped spark a revival. They eventually finished in eighteenth position, eight points clear of the relegation places.

It was hoped the improvement could continue into 1925-26 and initial optimism was justified, as United were second after seven games. However a terrible run of just two wins from fifteen left them bottom by the end of the year. There was an upturn in January with three straight wins but United could develop no consistency. When they lost three games over Easter without scoring a goal, their situation was desperate.

On the last day of the season United faced Tottenham at Elland Road, needing a win to guarantee survival. At half-time things looked bleak with the score level at 1-1 and rivals Burnley winning 3-0. In the second half however two goals from Jennings and one from Percy Whipp kept United in Division One.

Over the course of the season Jennings had been an ever present and scored 26 goals, the difference between survival and going down.

FACT 7

1927
GOALSCORING RECORDS
AND RELEGATION

When Leeds were relegated in 1926-27, they broke both their goals scored and goals conceded record.

After failing to win their first four games United recovered and were in the top half of the table for the whole of October and November. An impressive 4-1 home win over Sheffield Wednesday on 18th December meant United were eleventh going into Christmas.

There was then a disastrous fourteen game winless run. The last of these, a 6-2 loss at Sunderland, saw United sink to the bottom of the table with eight games remaining. Relegation was confirmed thanks to a 4-1 defeat at Tottenham on 23rd April, with two games still to go. By that time manager Arthur Fairclough had already offered his resignation but had been persuaded by the board to stay on until a successor was found.

Tom Jennings had again been in fine form, scoring 35 goals to break his own club goalscoring record. However their downfall was at the back, with departing captain Jim Baker not being adequately replaced. Changes in the offside rule meant there were plenty of goals across the Football League with United scoring 67 and conceded 88, both club records.

FACT 8

1928
DICK RAY LEADS LEEDS BACK UP

Following Arthur Fairclough's departure, Dick Ray returned to Leeds and led them to promotion at the first attempt, setting a goalscoring record in the process.

Ray had left United in 1923 to manage Doncaster Rovers in Division Three North. On returning to Elland Road, he didn't make any drastic changes to the side that had been relegated and managed to keep hold of the best players. He also brought in Charlie Keetley from non league Alvaston & Boulton.

United announced their intentions on the opening day of the season, winning 5-1 at South Shields. At Elland Road the goals flowed in, with United scoring five or more goals on four occasions before Christmas.

A 5-0 victory over Chelsea on 10th December was the start of a seven match winning run that lifted United from eighth to third. They suffered a setback with two defeats in February, but they then went on a twelve match unbeaten run, in which 26 goals were scored and just four conceded.

Promotion was clinched in the third from last game, with a 3-2 win over Chelsea at Stamford Bridge. However a home defeat to also promoted Manchester City the following week meant it was City who finished as champions.

United finished the season with 98 goals, which remains a club record today.

FACT 9

1930
A RECORD
FA CUP WIN

Leeds' record victory in the FA Cup happened on 11th January 1930 when Crystal Palace were thrashed 8-1.

Palace were in Division three South and had only won twice away from home all season. As part of their preparation for this tie, they spent a few days running around Epsom racecourse. The team were known for their fitness and pundits predicted that if they could keep United at bay, their stamina could help cause an upset.

On a snowy day it took United just five minutes to open the scoring through Russell Wainscoat. United were dominant and only the brilliance of the Palace keeper prevented them adding to the lead in the next half hour. John White finally got a second after 33 minutes and in the 37th minute Tom Jennings scored the third.

Six minutes into the second half Palace pulled a goal back but just a minute later Wainscoat made it 4-1. Wainscoat completed his hat-trick five minutes later and just after the hour mark Jennings scored the sixth. With fifteen minutes remaining Bobby Turnbull hit the seventh and the rout was completed five minutes later by White.

Any dreams of reaching Wembley were shattered in the next round, when United lost 4-1 at West Ham.

1931
RELEGATED

FACT 10

A year after finishing in their highest ever league position, Leeds United were relegated from Divison One.

United had finished fifth in 1929-30, having led the league in November. There were hopes they could again challenge for the championship and despite the loss of inside forward Jock White to Hearts, the squad was strong.

After failing to win their first three games, United picked up to win three of their next four. They could be in free scoring form one week but hopeless the next. A 7-3 win at Blackpool was followed by four successive defeats in which they scored just once, but then they beat Middlesbrough 7-0 at Elland Road.

Five games undefeated over Christmas and New Year lifted United to fifteenth but it was downhill from then on as they lost all four games in February to fall into the relegation zone. The FA Cup brought no comfort either as United were being embarrassed by a 3-1 defeat at Division Three South Exeter in the 5th round.

Three games unbeaten over Easter gave United hope but going into the final day of the season their fate was out of their hands. United beat Derby 3-1 at Elland Road but closest rivals were still condemned to the drop as closest rivals Blackpool snatched a point away at Manchester City.

FACT 11

1931
NINE WINS
IN A ROW

United's best winning sequence was back in the autumn of 1931 when they won nine matches in succession.

After relegation from the top flight United had a mixed start to the 1931-32 season, winning three and losing two of their first seven games. Then in the last game of September they beat Bristol City 2-0 away from home and followed this up with a 5-0 victory over Oldham at Elland Road.

There was then a comfortable 4-1 win at Bury before Wolves were beaten 2-1 at home. The fifth straight victory, 1-0 at Charlton, took United to the top of the league and they then had a 2-0 home win over Stoke.

A magnificent 5-2 win over Manchester United at Old Trafford made it seven out of seven and then Preston came to Elland Road and were thumped 4-1. United then had another big away win, beating Burnley 5-0.

The run finally came to an end on 29th November when Chesterfield snatched a 3-3 draw at Elland Road. By then however United had established themselves as favourites for promotion as they had a four point gap over their nearest rivals.

FACT 12

1932
PROMOTED
STRAIGHT BACK UP

United confirmed their reputation as a yo-yo club in 1931-32 when they were again promoted back to the top flight straight after relegation.

With Dick Ray still in charge United began the season strongly with two away wins but then lost two at home. However a 1-1 draw at Notts County on 12th September was the start of a fifteen match unbeaten run that took them to the top of the table.

There was a blow a week before Christmas when captain Willis Edwards was injured in a 2-1 defeat at Southampton. His absence was missed on Christmas Day in a 3-0 defeat at Bradford Park Avenue, but United recovered with three straight wins.

There was disappointment in the FA Cup when United were knocked out by QPR of Division Three South. However they remained focused in the league and a 3-2 win at fellow challengers Stoke on 12th March kept them at the top, six points ahead of third place.

United won only one of their next eight but they never dropped out of the top two. The nerves were finally settled in the penultimate game, when a 1-0 home win over Southampton secured promotion. United couldn't clinch the title though as they lost to Port Vale the following week, meaning they finished second to Wolves.

1934
RECORD LEAGUE WIN

FACT 13

On 7th April 1934 Leeds hammered Leicester City 8-0 to record what remains their record league win.

Going into the game United were twelfth in the table with Leicester two places below them. With both sides free of relegation worries it was expected to be a close game. The Yorkshire Post reported that the visitors were one of the most improved sides of late, while United had lost two in succession.

On a windy day it took United 28 minutes to open the scoring through Harry Duggan. Jack Mahon and Billy Furness then scored within a minute of each other and on the stroke of half-time Mahon made it 4-0.

Little more than a minute into the second half Furness got a fifth and on the hour Duggan scored from twenty five yards to put United 6-0 ahead. Soon afterwards Joe Firth struck United's seventh and he also rounded off the scoring with seventeen minutes left.

Leicester hadn't necessarily been that bad and had tested the keeper three times in the first fifteen minutes. However United, who were inspired by the return of Willis Edwards, took their chances superbly. They have not equalled this winning margin in the league since.

FACT 14
1934
A NEW KIT AND BADGE

For the 1934-35 season Leeds United abandoned their traditional blue and white stripes and also adopted a club crest to go with their new colours.

United first wore their new strip of gold and blue halves with white shorts for the sixth game of the season, at home to Liverpool on 22nd September 1934. They didn't bring any luck though as the visitors won 3-0. The shirts' colours came from the coat of arms of the city of Leeds and this was now used for the club's badge.

United remained in these colours until 1948 when manager Frank Buckley felt halved shirts made it difficult for players to pick one another out. After arranging a practice match with one side wearing halved shirts and the other plain, he persuaded the chairman to buy a set of plain gold shirts. There was another change in 1955, this time to plain blue.

The city coat of arms remained as the club crest until the early 1960s and there have been several changes since. The current design of a shield incorporating a ball inside a white rose and LUFC has been in use since 1999.

FACT 15

1935
BILLY HAMPSON
TAKES CHARGE

As Leeds once again struggled in the top flight, there was a managerial change in March 1935 with Billy Hampson taking over.

United struggled to maintain any consistency during the 1934-35 season. They were again knocked out of the FA Cup by lower division opposition, Division Two side Norwich City winning a replay at Elland Road.

On 5th March 1935 Dick Ray resigned. United were fourteenth in the table, but only three points clear of the relegation zone. The board appointed Ashington manager Billy Hampson, who had guested for Leeds City during World War One.

Hampson got off to the worst possible start, losing 7-1 at Chelsea, but they rallied to win three of their final six games to finish five points above relegated Leicester City.

The following season Hampson brought in some more experience to play alongside Ray's youngsters. His buys included George Brown, who had won league titles with Huddersfield, and keeper Albert McInroy, an FA Cup winner with Newcastle.

Hampson's blend helped United finish in a respectable eleventh place in 1935-36 and for the first time in six seasons attendances averaged 20,000.

FACT 16

1937
ANOTHER
GREAT ESCAPE

Leeds failed to build on the previous season's mid table finish and again fought relegation during 1936-37.

United failed to win any of their first four games and remained in the relegation places until the beginning of November, when three straight wins saw them rise up to seventeenth.

They continued to struggle without falling back into the drop zone. Results at Elland Road were satisfactory but away from home United were awful and lost nineteen out of their 21 games.

A disastrous run in March, when United lost five out of six games, saw them fall to the bottom of the table. Two wins from their next three games gave them some hope, but two successive defeats to Wolves saw them drop back to the bottom with two games left.

In their penultimate game United beat Sunderland 3-0 at home, meaning a point in their last match against Portsmouth, also at Elland Road, would ensure survival. A 3-1 triumph ensured United finished in nineteenth place to cling onto their Division One status but far better things had been expected of the side that season.

1938
GORDON HODGSON'S
FIVE GOALS

FACT 17

The only Leeds player to score five goals in a single game is Gordon Hodgson, who achieved the feat against Leicester in 1938-39.

South African Hodgson had been Liverpool's record scorer and joined United from Aston Villa in March 1937, shortly before his 32nd birthday. His six goals in thirteen appearances helped United avoid the drop and he continued his form into 1937-38, scoring 25 times in the league as United finished ninth.

On 1st October 1938 at Elland Road, Leicester City were desperately unlucky to lose their keeper Sandy McLaren through injury after thirty minutes. This meant they had to put defender Fred Sharman in goal and play with ten men. Within a minute of this happening Hodgson had scored, leading to Sharman handing the gloves to Billy Frame, but this still couldn't stop Hodgson completing his hat-trick before half-time.

In the second half things were evened up slightly when Jim Makinson left the field through injury. However Hodgson was still able to add to more as United ran out 8-2 winners. His five goals surpassed his own tally of four in a 4-4 draw against Everton the previous season. Hodgson finished the season with twenty goals, but the outbreak of World War Two brought his career to an end.

FACT 18

1939
THE RETURN OF WILF COPPING

A former crowd favourite returned to Leeds United in March 1939 leading to a turnaround in fortunes on the pitch, although matters were not quite the same off it.

Left-half Wilf Copping had joined Arsenal in the summer of 1934 and won two league titles and the FA Cup with the London club. However with the threat of war looming in March 1939, he asked to be transferred back to Yorkshire to be with his family.

Copping's first game back at United was a 2-0 defeat at Portsmouth, but on 11th March he starred in a 4-2 win over former club Arsenal at Elland Road. This was the first of three straight wins for United and helped ease any fears that they may be drawn into a relegation battle.

The United defence was much meaner after the arrival of Copping. After a run of 21 games in which they failed to keep a clean sheet, his presence in the side helped them prevent the opposition from scoring in five of the remaining twelve games. It meant United finished in thirteenth place, nine points clear of the relegation zone.

Unfortunately the war clouds were gathering in Europe and after just three games of the following season organised football was suspended after Britain declared war on Germany.

FACT 19

1944
ERIC STEPHENSON
KILLED IN ACTION

World War Two claimed the lives of one of Leeds' most promising players when Eric Stephenson was killed whilst fighting in Burma.

Stephenson, an inside left, joined United as an amateur in 1933 and broke into the side on a regular basis during the 1936-37 season. In 1938 he earned his first international cap, appearing for England against Scotland at Wembley.

By the time war broke out in September 1939 Stephenson had played for United 111 times, scoring 21 goals. He first enlisted as a physical training instructor, enabling him to appear for United in the regionalised wartime competitions. However in 1942 he joined the Gurkha Rifles and was part of a unit that advanced into Japanese held Burma.

Stephenson was fighting in a dangerous campaign in the jungle and he was killed on 8th September 1944, four days after his thirtieth birthday. When peace came, United played Celtic in a benefit game with the proceeds going to his widow. His daughter Jan has published a biography of him, entitled *The Happy Warrior; From Leeds United to Burma*.

Other United players to lose their lives during World War Two were Maurice Hubert Lawn, Vernon Allen, Leslie Thompson and Robert Montgomery.

FACT 20

1947
WORST AWAY RECORD
IN TOP FLIGHT HISTORY

When the Football League resumed after World War Two, it was a forgettable campaign for Leeds. In 1946-47 they were relegated with a record low points haul from away matches.

There was little money available for transfers and manager Billy Hampson relied mainly on the pre war squad. However they were past their prime and after just one win from the opening eight games United were bottom at the end of September.

Two successive home wins at the beginning of October lifted United out of the bottom three but they couldn't pick up anything away from home. After ten successive away defeats, they finally managed a 1-1 draw at Brentford on 30th November.

United were unable to build on that first away point and by the New Year they were back at the bottom of the table. For the rest of the season they were never off it and after beating Chelsea 2-1 at Elland Road on 18th January, they failed to win any of their remaining seventeen games.

The inevitable relegation was confirmed on 26th April with a 2-1 defeat at Derby when there were still five games to go. They finished the season with just eighteen points and just one point from 21 games remains an all time record low in the top flight.

FACT 21

1948
MAJOR FRANK BUCKLEY

After coming close to dropping down to Division Three in 1947-48 Leeds changed their approach to hiring managers and appointed Major Frank Buckley.

When Billy Hampson resigned following relegation, former captain Willis Edwards became manager. After finishing in eighteenth place, he was relieved of his duties and given a scouting role.

The United board decided to look for a manager with no previous club connection and appointed 64 year old Major Frank Buckley, a veteran of the Boer War and World War One. Buckley had managed Wolverhampton Wanderers between 1927 and 1944, winning promotion to Division One, finishing runners up and also reaching an FA Cup final.

Buckley was well ahead of his time and known for his authoritarian style and his ability to handle the media. He was also shrewd in the transfer market and could develop youth. In December 1948 he signed John Charles, who would become one of the club's greatest ever players.

Amongst the innovative new ideas Buckley introduced were dancing in training and the use of mechanical devices to help practice ball technique. United finished fifteenth in Buckley's first season and they then challenged for promotion three seasons running. He resigned after finishing tenth in 1952-53, believing he could not achieve promotion with the funds available. He was replaced by Raich Carter.

1953
JACK CHARLTON'S DEBUT

FACT 22

In his last game in charge Major Frank Buckley gave a debut to another promising youngster who would go on to be a Leeds United great.

Jack Charlton was two weeks away from his eighteenth birthday when he was selected to play in defence for the last game of the season away to Doncaster Rovers on 25th April 1953. Charlton later said that the first he knew about it was seeing his name on the dressing room door the day before the game and that he was given no instructions on how to play.

Doncaster took the lead midway through the first half but Eric Kerfoot rescued a point for United twelve minutes from time. Charlton had come into the side in place of Jim McCabe and the *Yorkshire Post* reported that he 'played well enough to be noted for the future at centre-half.'

Charlton spent the next two years on National Service and only appeared once. However when he returned to the side in 1955-56 he helped United to promotion and would become a key figure in the glory years. When he finally retired in 1973, he had played for the club 762 times.

FACT 23

1953 FLOODLIGHT SWITCH ON

When floodlights were first installed at Elland Road in 1953 they were the most expensive in the Football League.

The lights were installed at a cost of £7,000 and the first match to be played under them was on 9th November 1953 when Hibernian were the visitors to Elland Road. The attendance of 31,500 was the biggest of the season so far and they were greeted by lights described by the Yorkshire Post reporter as the brightest he had ever seen.

The game may have been a friendly but it had an extremely competitive edge, with play being at top speed and tackles flying in from all angles. The game was so physical that John Charles had to go off injured after an hour, needing two stitches to a cut above the eye.

By the time Charles had gone off he had scored two of United's goals in what turned out to be a 4-1 win. The other two were scored by manager Raich Carter, the 39 year old using the game as an opportunity to name himself in the line-up.

The lights were in use until 1974 when they were replaced by the tallest in Europe, which stood at 260 feet tall.

FACT 24

1954
RECORD GOAL HAUL

In 1953-54 John Charles created a club scoring record that still stands today.

Fourteen games into the previous season Charles had been switched from centre half to centre forward by Major Frank Buckley. The move was an instant success and he finished the campaign with 27 goals from 29 league and cup matches.

Raich Carter continued with Charles at centre forward and on the opening day of 1953-53 he hit four in a 6-0 win over Notts County at Elland Road. The following week he got another hat-trick against Rotherham in a 4-2 home victory.

Before Christmas Charles had got two more hat-tricks, in a 4-4 draw at Bury and 4-2 win at Rotherham. On 27th March 1954 he scored in a 4-2 defeat at Oldham. This was his 36th league goal of the season and broke Tom Jennings' record which had been set in 1936-37.

Charles struck six goals in his final four matches to finish the season on 42 from 39 appearances. It is a goalscoring record that has not been matched by any United player since.

1954
LEEDS UNITED'S
OLDEST PLAYER

FACT 25

The oldest player to appear for United was Eddie Burbanks, who made his debut for the club after his fortieth birthday.

With winger George Meek away on National Service for a year, Raich Carter signed Burbanks at the beginning of the 1953-54 season. He had been

born on 1st April 1913 and played alongside Carter for Sunderland in the 1937 FA Cup final, scoring the winning goal.

Burbanks, who had guested for United in World War Two, started the first twelve games of the season at left wing. However he failed to make any great impact and scored only one goal. He lost his place to Arthur Lynch and had to spend the rest of the season in the reserves.

Burbanks was recalled to the first team for the final game of the season away to another of his previous clubs, Hull, on 24th April 1954. He was named captain and the match ended in a 1-1 draw, meaning United finished the season in tenth place.

After retiring from playing, Burbanks returned to live in Hull where he ran a sweet shop. He died in 1983.

FACT 26

1956
PROMOTION
FINALLY ACHIEVED

Leeds finally won promotion in 1955-56, a year after just missing out.

The 1954-55 season saw one of the closest ever promotion races, with United finishing fourth but just a point behind the champions. They began the following campaign as one of the favourites but had a mixed start. After ten games they were in eighth place but only three points behind leaders Bristol Rovers.

Manager Raich Carter made a tactical change in October by moving John Charles, who had been covering for injuries in midfield, back into attack. The extra strength led to more consistency, especially at Elland Road and by New Year they had risen up to third.

There was then a disappointing run of one win from nine games. After the Easter period United were eighth with six games remaining. Sheffield Wednesday had all but secured promotion but only two points separated United from second placed Liverpool.

On 2nd April Charles hit a hat-trick as Fulham were thrashed 6-1 and four more wins lifted United to second with one game left. On the last day of the season, United travelled to Hull knowing a draw would be enough to take them up. They made no mistake though, winning 4-1 to return to Division One after a nine year absence.

FACT 27

1956
FIRE IN THE
WEST STAND

Optimism surrounding Leeds' promising start in the top flight was ruined when the West Stand was destroyed by fire.

United won six of their opening nine games and were second in the table. However in the early hours of 18th September 1956 the West Stand was engulfed in flames, destroying the club offices, records, changing rooms, directors' box and press room. The flames were so bad that even the pitch was scorched and all that was left was the stand's metal framework.

Despite the damage, the following Saturday's fixture at home to Aston Villa still went ahead. Raich Carter ordered a supply of new boots and injured players were treated at the home of the physio. The players changed at a local sports club before being bussed to Elland Road and the press sat on benches along the touchline.

United took the lead shortly before half-time thanks to a goal from John Charles, who hit a fine shot after chesting down a cross from Bobby Forrest. The players then went back to their bus for refreshment and tactical talks, but there were no further goals after the break.

United went on to finish in a respectable seventh place and the following season a brand new stand was unveiled at a cost of £180,000.

FACT 28

1957
A WORLD TRANSFER RECORD

One of the consequences of paying for the new West Stand was that Leeds had to sell John Charles. However they did receive a world record transfer fee for their best asset.

United had always resisted offers for Charles but as he continued his scoring exploits in Division One, Europe's top clubs began to show an interest. Knowing the money was needed towards the stand the directors decided in April that although they would not sell to an English club, Charles was free to move abroad.

Real Madrid and Inter Milan were keen but Juventus were the first club to make a firm offer. Eventually a fee of £65,000 was agreed, a world record at the time, and he was allowed to play in the last few games of the season.

Charles said his farewells against Sunderland at Elland Road on 22nd April. He scored the second and third goals in a 3-1 victory. They were his 37th and 38th of the season and the *Yorkshire Post* reported that he could 'not have made a more fitting end to his career at Elland Road.'

FACT 29

1958
RAICH CARTER LEAVES

After finishing seventeenth in Division One the Leeds board decided against renewing manager Raich Carter's contract, a move that surprised most of the football world.

United struggled to adapt to life without John Charles and were in the bottom half of the table all season. Hugh Baird was signed from Airdrie for £12,000 to replace Charles but as the difference between the two players fees suggested, he was nowhere near the same class.

At the end of November United fell into the relegation zone after five successive defeats and remained there or thereabouts for the next four months.

A 3-0 defeat at Preston on 15th March saw United fall to second bottom with nine games left. However they rallied and lost just once more all season, eventually finishing five points clear of the drop zone.

Carter maintained he had done the best he could with limited resources as he had not been allowed to spend all of the fee received for Charles. However with his five year contract up for renewal, the board decided not to give him an extension which was a surprising one.

Trainer Bill Lambton was promoted to manager. Carter was so stunned by the decision that he stayed away for the game for eighteen months until January 1960 when he became manager of Mansfield.

1960
BILLY BREMNER'S DEBUT

FACT 30

The man who would captain Leeds to some of their greatest triumphs made his debut as a seventeen year old on 23rd January 1960.

Bremner's opportunity to play away to Chelsea came as regular right winger Chris Crowe was doing his National Service and was required for an army fixture. Veteran Don Revie took Bremner under his wing, sharing a room with him and taking him for a long walk on the morning of the game.

The two players formed a good understanding on the right in a game that United won 3-1. Bremner missed the next few games but was recalled to the side, scoring his first goal in a 3-3 draw with Birmingham on 9th March. He progressed so quickly that before the end of the season Cowley was sold to Blackburn.

The development of Bremner, who went on to play 773 times for the club, was one of the few positives from the season. Bill Lambton had been replaced as manager in the summer by Jack Taylor, but he was unable to arrest the slide.

United dropped into the relegation zone following a 3-0 defeat against Wolves on 2nd April. There were still eight games left but they never looked like staying up and their goals against tally of 92 was the worst in the division.

FACT 31
1961
THE APPOINTMENT OF DON REVIE

Don Revie was a surprise appointment as Leeds United manager in 1961, having looked set to be seeking a new challenge elsewhere.

By the beginning of the 1960-61 season Revie was now 33 years old and his best years as a player were behind him. As Jack Taylor tried to find the best combination, Revie was in and out of the team and he could not put a consistent run of form together.

Revie's last appearance of the season was on 14th January 1961 when United beat Southampton 3-0 at Elland Road. During February and March United struggled and lost four games in succession. Revie watched from the sidelines whilst applying for player manager job at Bournemouth and also attracting interest from Chester, Tranmere and Australian side Adamstown.

On 11th March United beat Norwich 1-0 to end their losing run but Taylor had, had enough and resigned a few days later. Revie was then persuaded by director Harold Reynolds to reconsider and apply for the United job instead.

It was a big gamble with United struggling in Division Two but Reynolds was able to persuade the rest of the board to appoint Revie on a three year contract. There would later be no doubt that they had made the right decision.

1961
ALBERT JOHANNESON

FACT 32

In 1961 Leeds signed a player who hailed from a South African township and became one of the first high profile black footballers in England.

Albert Johanneson was recommended to United by a teacher who had seen him play for Germiston Colliers in South Africa. He was given a trial by United in January 1961 and after impressing made his debut for the club that April. He was not the first black player to play for United — that was Gerry Francis, with whom Johanneson played just one game, but Francis was never a regular.

Johanneson was a skilful left winger who could go past defenders with ease. He was given the nickname of the Black Flash and helped Leeds to promotion in 1964, then became the first black player to appear in the FA Cup final in 1965. However he was often subject to racist abuse from opposition fans and sometimes players as well—getting little protection from referees.

He joined York City from United in 1970 having scored 67 goals in 197 games. After retiring from playing he suffered from alcoholism and depression and eventually died a recluse at his Leeds home in 1995.

FACT 33
1961
ALL WHITE

As Don Revie prepared for his first full season as manager he set about making some big changes at the club, including abandoning the traditional kit.

United had worn blue and gold for forty years but Revie felt that a line should be drawn under the past as they looked to a new future. This meant an all white strip, in direct imitation of Real Madrid who had won the European Cup five years running between 1956 and 1960.

Revie also changed the wage structure, putting all players on the same basic pay but with incentive based bonuses based on appearances, wins and attendances.

In the boardroom, Revie was backed by the increasingly influential Harry Reynolds, who insisted that if the team were to be a top club they had to act like one. This meant better travel arrangements and higher quality hotels when the team went on away trips.

Despite all the enthusiasm, supporters were not convinced. Only 12,916 turned out to see the opening game of the season against Charlton. Billy Bremner scored the only goal as United won 1-0 and in midweek they beat Brighton 3-1 away from home. However the following Saturday they were brought right back down to earth, losing 5-0 against Liverpool at Anfield.

FACT 34

1962
BOBBY COLLINS HELPS UNITED AVOID DROP

Leeds looked to be heading for Division Three in 1961-62 until a new signing helped them avoid the drop.

The early season optimism soon went away and by the end of September United were in the relegation zone after a run of six defeats in seven games.

United were woefully inconsistent and unpredictable. A 3-1 defeat at bottom club Charlton on 16th December was followed a week later by a 1-0 win over leaders Liverpool. On 24th February a 3-2 home defeat to Plymouth saw United sink to the bottom of the table.

When they lost 4-1 at Southampton on 17th March, United were three points from safety with nine games left. However, Don Revie had the previous week made the brave decision to sign Scottish international Bobby Collins from Everton for a club record £25,000.

Collins made a huge difference, with United winning two and drawing six of the next eight games. However to be sure of staying up they had to win at Newcastle in their final game, although their superior goal average meant a draw would probably do. There was no need to worry though as goals from Albert Johanneson and Billy McAdams, as well as an own goal, saw United cruise to a 3-0 victory.

1963
REVIE'S BABES

FACT 35

John Charles returned to Leeds for the 1962-63 season but he was overshadowed by the emergence of youth.

United broke their transfer record in the summer of 1962 to bring Charles, who was now 31 years old, back to Elland Road. They then had a mixed start, winning two and losing three of the first six games.

For the trip to Swansea on 8th September, Don Revie took a brave step and brought four teenagers into the side. They

were keeper Gary Sprake, Paul Reaney, Norman Hunter and centre forward Rodney Johnson, who replaced the injured Charles. United won 2-0, with the Yorkshire Post reporting that they had been faster and more accurate than in any other game.

Charles returned for the next game at home to promotion favourites Chelsea, but the other three teenagers kept their places in a 2-0 win. However the Welshman was struggling to adapt to the physical demands of Division Two. After just three goals in ten games, he returned to Italy in November to join Roma.

As the season progressed more teenagers were given their chance, including Peter Lorimer who became the clubs youngest player aged just fifteen years and 289 days. United enjoyed a good second half of the season and finished fourth, just four points off the promotion places.

FACT 36

1964
DIVISION TWO
CHAMPIONS

Leeds returned to the top flight after a four year absence. In their promotion season they lost just one of their opening eight games, but four draws meant they were sixth in the table. They then won five in succession, taking them to the top. A magnificent run of form saw United remain unbeaten until 28th December, when they lost 2-0 at fellow contenders Sunderland.

A six game unbeaten run followed, but United then lost 2-0 at third placed Preston on 3rd March. This meant they remained in second, but now only on goal average. It would be United's last defeat of the season however and four straight wins saw them overtake Sunderland.

Promotion was secured with a 3-0 win at Swansea on 11th April. The following Saturday the players ran around the pitch with a banner thanking fans for their support, but they then stumbled to a 1-1 draw with relegation threatened Plymouth. This meant Sunderland drew level on points in the battle for the championship trophy.

United were desperate to go up as champions and a week later they secured the trophy with a 2-0 win at Swansea. They finished the season having lost just three games and with the highest Division Two points total since Tottenham in 1920.

FACT 37

1964
THE BEST PERFORMANCE SINCE THE WAR

Leeds' first home game back in Division One saw them beat champions Liverpool 4-2. The performance was described as their best since World War 2.

United beat Aston Villa 2-1 away from home on the opening day, but Don Revie warned that Liverpool would be a far tougher test.

Albert Johanneson's sixteenth minute shot from eighteen yards deflected off Ron Yeats to put United ahead. Eight minutes later Roger Hunt headed Liverpool level and it was feared their class could take over, but United refused to let them settle. They fought for every ball, switched attackers between positions and five minutes before half-time Don Weston scored with a header from Jim Storrie's cross.

In the second half United tore into the Reds from the kickoff and scored two more within ten minutes, the goals coming from Billy Bremner and Johnny Giles. With twenty minutes to go Liverpool were awarded a penalty and although Gary Sprake saved Gordon Milne's kick, he scored from the rebound.

The victory was attributed to Revie's refusal to allow his players to be in awe of Liverpool. It was a team effort and although United fought hard, they played attractive football too. The *Yorkshire Evening Post's* Phil Brown said that it was the best football that they had played since the war.

FACT 38

1965
SO CLOSE TO THE TITLE

United's first season back in Division One was their best ever to date as they missed out on the title only on goal average.

After winning their first three games, United wobbled in September and won only two out of eight. They followed this up though with seven straight wins to lift them to third. They went top for the first time on 2nd January, with a 2-1 win over Sunderland at Elland Road.

That win was part of an eighteen game unbeaten run. Going into Easter United were three points clear with five games remaining. However a 1-0 home defeat to closest challengers Manchester United threw the race wide open. Two days later, on Easter Monday, they lost 3-0 at Sheffield Wednesday and fell to second.

United won their next two games but the title was now out of their hands. In their last game on 26th April, United were 3-0 down to already relegated Birmingham but managed to fight back to draw 3-3. The only way United could win the league now was if Manchester United lost 17-0 at Aston Villa two nights later. They did lose 2-1 but although it had been a tremendous effort by United they had fallen short at the final hurdle.

FACT 39

1965
THE FIRST
FA CUP FINAL

Leeds reached their first FA Cup final in 1964-65 but just as in the league that season, they couldn't quite do enough to lift the trophy.

Wins over Southport, Everton, Shrewsbury and Crystal Palace took United to the semi-final for the first time. They drew 0-0 with Manchester United at Hillsborough then in the replay at Nottingham Forest's City ground an 89th minute header from Billy Bremner took United to Wembley.

The opponents for the final were Liverpool, who were also seeking to win the FA Cup for the first time. It was the Reds though who showed less nerves and although it was 0-0 after ninety minutes, it was down to the form of United keeper Gary Sprake.

Early in extra time Roger Hunt scored for Liverpool but Billy Bremner scored with a superb volley to bring United level. However in the second period Ian St John scored again for Liverpool and there was no way back for United now.

United had suffered a double disappointment, but it had been a season when Bobby Collins was outstanding and Jack Charlton and Billy Bremner were capped by their countries. They had qualified for European competition for the first time and were undoubtedly now one of English football's top sides.

FACT 40
1966 EUROPEAN SEMI-FINALISTS

Leeds first entry into European competition saw them reach the semi-finals, where they lost to Real Zaragoza in a playoff.

Finishing second in the league meant United qualified for the Inter Cities Fairs Cup, a forerunner to the UEFA Cup and Europa League. They defeated Torino, SC Leipzig, Valencia and Ujpest Dozsa get to the last four, where they were paired with 1964 winners Real Zaragoza.

The first leg in Spain was fiercely contested and the only goal came from a hotly disputed penalty, awarded after the referee adjudged Billy Bremner to have handballed. Gary Sprake got a hand to the kick but the ball went in off the post.

Don Revie was confident of turning the tie around at Elland Road and Albert Johanneson bundled the ball over the line midway through the first half. However on the hour Canario equalised for Zaragoza, but within three minutes Jack Charlton had scored with a header to level the tie.

There were no away goals or penalties to settle games so a coin was tossed to decide the venue for a replay. United won but two weeks later the Elland Road crowd was shellshocked as the spaniards raced into a 3-0 lead after just fourteen minutes. Charlton did manage a consolation but Revie had to admit United had been outplayed.

1967
RECORD ATTENDANCE

FACT 41

Leeds' record attendance came in an FA Cup fifth round replay in March 1967 when almost 58,000 squeezed into Elland Road.

After drawing 1-1 at Roker Park, United and Sunderland faced each other again at Elland Road four days later. There was huge interest in the game, with a rivalry having developed between the two clubs during the 1964 promotion battle.

Due to the time factor the game wasn't all ticket and the ground was dangerously overcrowded. During the first half play was stopped for seventeen minutes when crush barriers collapsed on the popular side,

leading to 1,000 fans spilling onto the pitch. 32 people were taken to hospital and it was a miracle nobody was killed or seriously injured.

Sunderland took the lead against the run of play in the 35th minute but Johnny Giles equalised almost from the restart. The game went to extra time but the visitors defence was outstanding and United couldn't find a way through.

The official attendance was announced at 57,892 which was 5,000 more than the ground's capacity at the time. Given what had happened with the barriers, the second replay at Hull City's Boothferry Park was declared all ticket and United won 2-1 thanks to a late Giles penalty.

FACT 42

1967
WINNING WITH
A COIN TOSS

In 1966-67 Leeds reached the final of the Fairs Cup with the help of the toss of a coin after their quarter final tie finished all square.

After receiving a bye in the first round United were drawn against Dutch side DWS Amsterdam, winning comfortably 3-1 in Holland and 5-1 at home. In the third round they drew 1-1 at home to Valencia before winning the away leg 2-0 in Spain.

The quarter final draw paired United with Italian side Bologna. After losing 1-0 away United won by the same scoreline at Elland Road but there were no penalty shoot-outs back then. It meant the referee had to toss a coin to decide who went through and it landed on the United side.

United faced Scottish side Kilmarnock in the semi-final, winning 4-2 at home then drawing 0-0 away. The final against Dinamo Zagreb was held over to the beginning of the next season and in the first leg United lost 2-0 away from home. Back at Elland Road a week later they were unable to overturn this deficit, drawing 0-0.

FACT 43

1968
END OF THE
TROPHY FAMINE

After the disappointments of the last three seasons Leeds finally claimed a first major trophy in 1967-68 when they won the League Cup.

United beat Luton and Bury at home before travelling to Sunderland and winning 2-0 at Roker Park. In the fifth round they beat Stoke 2-0 at Elland Road, setting up a semi-final with Derby County. United won 1-0 at the Baseball Ground then 3-2 at Elland Road.

The final was only the second in the League Cup to take place at Wembley and United's opponents were Arsenal, who hadn't played at the national stadium since 1952.

Both sides were cautious but in the twentieth minute Terry Cooper seized on a loose ball and scored from long range. United then shut up shop and Arsenal didn't have the skill to breach their defence.

Revie came in for some criticism from the media for the tactics. However following the disappointments of recent years, it was inevitable that no unnecessary risks would be taken. Both Jimmy Greenhoff and Johnny Giles had been carrying injuries and Giles especially struggled to make a contribution.

It hadn't been the most entertaining final but nobody at Elland Road was complaining. The nearly men tag had finally been shaken off.

FACT 44

1968
FIRST BRITISH TEAM
TO WIN FAIRS CUP

After their League Cup triumph in 1967-68 Leeds added a second trophy a few months later, becoming the first English team to win the Fairs Cup.

United had an easy start, beating Spora Luxembourg 16-0 on aggregate, the 9-0 away leg win remaining a club record victory on the road. The second round was a much closer affair, United beating Partizan Belgrade 3-2 over two legs.

In the third round a narrow 1-0 home win over Hibernian was followed by a 1-1 draw in Edinburgh. United then beat Rangers in the quarter final, drawing 0-0 at Ibrox and winning 2-0 at Elland Road. United faced a Scottish side again in the semi-final, drawing 1-1 with Dundee at Dens Park then winning 1-0 at home.

The final was held back until August. In the first leg at Elland Road, Hungarians Ferencvaros were content to sit back and defend. Four minutes before half-time Mick Jones scored but United couldn't add to this and had to make do with a slender 1-0 lead to take into the second leg.

In front of 76,000 fans at the Nep Stadium in Budapest, they remained strong at the back to hold out for a 0-0 draw and make up for the disappointment of 1967.

FACT 45

1969
RECORDS TUMBLE
ON WAY TO TITLE

Leeds became champions of the Football League for the first time in 1968-69, breaking a number of records along the way.

United swept all before them, losing just two out of their 42 league games, a new record. One of those defeats was a 5-1 hammering at Burnley but United made up for it at Elland Road, winning 6-1.

Early defeats in all the cup competitions may have helped United's cause as they were left to concentrate on the league.

On 28th April United faced Liverpool at Anfield in their penultimate game, knowing a win or draw would be enough to secure the title. Liverpool still had an outside chance themselves and threw everything they could at united, but Alun Evans missed two great opportunities.

United held on for a 0-0 draw and then there were unforgettable scenes as the home fans applauded them as worthy champions. Two nights later United beat Nottingham Forest 1-0 in front of an ecstatic Elland Road crowd. With only two points for a win back then, this meant they finished the season on 67 points, breaking Arsenal's record set in 1931.

Other records broken were the most wins, most home points and most home wins. A curious record though was that United only scored 66 goals, the lowest by a title winning side since the offside law was changed in 1925.

FACT 46

1969
LEEDS UNITED 10
LYN OSLO 0

Leeds' first ever match in the European Cup ended in a club record 10-0 victory over Lyn Oslo.

The Norwegian part timers played six at the back but it took United just 35 seconds to unlock their defence. Mike O'Grady scored from a fierce shot and before ten minutes was up Mick Jones had added two more.

Allan Clarke got the fourth midway through the half and Eddie Gray's thirty yard drive in the 34th minute made it 5-0. The score remained that way until half-time but there was no let up after the break from United, with Clarke heading a sixth soon after the restart.

Johnny Giles scored from thirty yards for the seventh and soon after the hour mark, Jones completed his hat-trick from a similar distance, his shot going in off the post. In the 65th minute Billy Bremner got in on the act, making it 9-0 from outside the box.

An injury to Giles disrupted the team a little but with seconds remaining United got their tenth. Bremner tried a shot from distance which deflected into the goal off a defender to set a new record victory for United that still stands today. United won the second leg 6-0 and went on to reach the semi-final.

1970
EUROPEAN CROWD RECORD

FACT 47

When Leeds faced Celtic in Glasgow in the second leg of the European Cup semi-final on 15th April 1970, they did so in front of a record crowd in European club competition.

Celtic, aiming to reach a second European Cup final in four years, switched the game to Hampden Park which was the largest stadium in Europe at the time. United trailed 1-0 from the first leg and were allocated 10,000 tickets, but half of them were returned and quickly snapped up by Celtic fans.

Despite Celtic dominating early on and forcing six corners in the first eight minutes, it was United that scored first. Billy Bremner's shot from thirty yards went in off the angle of post and bar to level the tie and silence the vast majority of the crowd.

It remained 1-0 at half-time but two minutes after the restart John Hughes headed in Celtic's equaliser from a corner. United were then dealt a massive blow when keeper Gary Sprake was injured and had to be carried off. His replacement David Harvey had only been on the pitch three minutes when Bobby Murdoch put Celtic 3-1 ahead on aggregate to end United hopes of reaching the final.

The official attendance was 136,505, a record for European competition that is unlikely ever to be beaten.

FACT 48

1970
UNITED BLOW TREBLE CHANCE

In 1969-70 Leeds looked on course for a Treble but ended up with nothing after winning just one of their last ten games.

Approaching the end of March United had played 52 games in all competitions and suffered only three defeats. However Everton pushed them all the way in the title race and clinched the championship on 1st April.

In the European Cup, United were beaten 1-0 at home by Celtic in the first leg of the semi-final. In between then and the second leg, they drew 2-2 with Chelsea in the FA Cup final at Wembley, the Chelsea equaliser coming two minutes from time.

United's elimination from Europe was confirmed when they lost 2-1 to Celtic in the second leg of the European Cup final on 15th April. A fortnight later they had the opportunity to salvage something from the season when they faced Chelsea in the FA Cup final replay. However Chelsea came from behind to win 2-1 in extra time.

United were arguably the best team in the country but had been left empty handed. The impending World Cup in Mexico was a factor, as the season ended far earlier than usual. They also weren't helped by a marathon FA Cup semi-final tie with Manchester United, which was only settled after two replays.

FACT 49
1971
AWAY GOALS RULES

When Leeds won the Fairs Cup for the second time in 1970-71 they became the first side to win a European trophy thanks to the away goals rule.

United enjoyed a comfortable 6-0 aggregate victory over Sarpsborg in the first round, but needed away goals to beat Dynamo Dresden, winning 1-0 at home and losing 2-1 in East Germany.

In the third round United hammered Sparta Prague 6-0 at home then won 3-2 away. They followed this up with a narrow 3-2 win on aggregate over Portuguese side Vitoria Setubal in the quarter-final.

The semi-final was an all English affair, United winning 1-0 against Liverpool at Anfield and then drawing 1-1 at Elland Road.

The first leg of the final against Juventus in Turin was abandoned after an hour due to torrential rain with the score at 0-0. Two days later the side met again, with United coming from 2-0 down to draw 2-2 thanks to goals from Paul Madeley and Mick Bates. Back at Elland Road Allan Clarke scored early on and Anastasi equalised, there was no further scoring in extra time United were confirmed as winners thanks to the away goals rule.

United's triumph also meant that they had become the first English team to win a European trophy more than once.

1971
REFEREE BLUNDER ENDS TITLE HOPES

FACT 50

Leeds' hopes of becoming champions of the Football League in 1970-71 were dashed when an inexplicable refereeing decision led to them losing 2-1 against West Bromwich Albion at Elland Road.

On 17th April United were two points ahead of Arsenal but had played two games more. Trailing 1-0 with just under half an hour left, Albion's Tony Brown intercepted a pass and ran into the United half with Colin Suggett supporting him. The linesman flagged for offside against Suggett and even though Brown had stopped, referee Ray Tinkler waved play on.

Brown then took the ball forward and squared to Jeff Astle, who appeared offside. Despite the appeals of the United defenders, no flag was raised and Astle put the visitors 2-0 ahead. There was then chaos as the United players surrounded the referee and then had to protect him from irate fans who ran onto the pitch.

United pulled a goal back but this 2-1 defeat, coupled with Arsenal's victory over Newcastle, gave the Gunners the title advantage.

When the season ended United finished a point behind Arsenal and their points haul of 64 was the highest ever by a second placed side.

FACT 51

1971
ASA HARTFORD'S
MOVE BREAKS DOWN

In November 1971 Leeds looked set to sign a player they believed would help them win the title, but the transfer fell through on medical advice.

At the beginning of the month Don Review agreed a club record fee of £177,000 to buy West Bromwich Albion's attacking midfielder Asa Hartford. The 21 year old had just been called up by Scotland for the first time and was described by the *Yorkshire Post* as 'a level headed young man with a mind of his own.'

Hartford looked set to make his debut against Leicester at Elland Road on 5th November but hours before the game the deal was off. A statement from club secretary Brian Archer said he had failed a medical examination. There was no further comment from Hartford or Revie and United went on to win 2-1.

It later transpired that Hartford had a pin sized hole in his heart. He had been born with it and it hadn't affected his career to date, but medical officials felt it was too risky given the size of the fee.

United finished the season in second place, just a point behind champions Derby County. Nobody knows what would have happened had the transfer gone ahead, but Hartford went on to enjoy a lengthy career with Manchester City and Everton.

FACT 52

1972
FA CUP WINNERS

After twice being beaten finalists Leeds finally won the FA Cup in 1972, but two nights later they were unable to complete the Double.

United had a tough route to the final, knocking out Liverpool and Tottenham on the way to Wembley where their opponents were holders Arsenal.

It was a hard fought game with the first foul coming within five seconds of kick-off when United's Allan Clarke obstructed Alan Ball. Both sides cancelled each other out in midfield and United's best chance in the first half was when Clarke had a header come back off the bar.

The deadlock was finally broken in the 53rd minute when Mick Jones crossed and Clarke stooped to head home to send the United fans wild. Arsenal almost equalised in the 69th minute when Charlie George's shot came off the bar but Peter Simpson hit the rebound over.

United held on to win and the cup was presented by the Queen to Billy Bremner. Two days later however, they missed the chance to secure the Double. Needing to win at Wolves to clinch the league title, they lost 2-1 meaning Derby County were the champions.

FACT 53

1973 CUP WINNERS CUP SCANDAL

When United were beaten finalists in the 1972-73 European Cup Winners Cup, questions were raised about the integrity of the referee.

United had a narrow 2-1 aggregate victory over Turkish side Ankaragucu in the first round then beat East Germans Carl Zeiss Jena 2-0 over the two legs. In the quarter final they comfortably disposed of Rapid Bucharest, 5-0 at home and 3-1 away.

The semi-final against Yugoslavs Hajduck Split was a close affair, United winning 1-0 at home then drawing 0-0 away.

The final against AC Milan took place in the Greek city of Salonika. Chiarugi scored for the Italians from a disputed free kick after three minutes and United were frustrated by Milan's defensive tactics for the rest of the game. They weren't helped by the Greek referee Michas who turned down three clear penalty appeals, one for handball and the other two for fouls.

At the end of the game the winners were jeered by the Greek fans who chanted 'Shame'. Despite protests UEFA refused to carry out a formal investigation, even though some Greek football officials had raised concerns over the appointment of a referee who had Italian connections.

FACT 54

1974
RECORD BREAKING
RUN TO TITLE

When Leeds won their second Football League Championship in 1973-74, they set a new record for the most games unbeaten from the start of a season.

United won their first seven matches and kept going unbeaten to surpass Sheffield United's record of 23 games without defeat from the start of a season. They looked set to equal Burnley's record of thirty games unbeaten at any stage of a campaign, only to lose 3-2 to Stoke on 23rd February, their thirtieth match.

A surprise FA Cup defeat to Bristol City in the fifth round allowed United to concentrate on the league. However three successive defeats in March, including one to closest challengers Liverpool meant the race looked set to go to the wire.

United's form picked up again in April and when they beat Ipswich 3-2 at Elland Road in their final home game it meant victory at QPR the following week would secure the title. However on 24th April Liverpool lost at home to Arsenal to hand the title to United on the same night Don Revie was featured on ITV's *This is Your Life*.

Despite having already been crowned champions, United maintained their professionalism and won the last game of the season 1-0 at Loftus Road, meaning they finished five points clear of Liverpool.

FACT 55

1974
BRIAN CLOUGH'S
44 DAYS

When Don Revie left Leeds to take the England job, his high profile replacement remained at Elland Road for only 44 days.

A Football League Championship winner with Derby in 1972, Brian Clough was given a five year contract by United chairman Manny Cussins, who described him as the ideal manager.

Clough set out to make his mark early on, transfer listing established players and imposing a harsh discipline regime. After losing on penalties against Liverpool in the Charity Shield, United lost their opening league game 3-0 at Stoke.

United managed just one win in their first six games under Clough. He was sacked after a 1-1 home draw with newly promoted Luton on 7th September, a result that left them nineteenth in the table.

Clough had been in the job just 44 days and Cussins said the club and happiness of the players had to come first. Clough said it was a sad day for the club amidst press reports that the players had revolted against him.

Jimmy Armfield agreed to replace Clough, who took over at Nottingham Forest the following January and took them from Division Two to European Cup winners.

1975 EUROPEAN CUP FINAL HEARTBREAK

FACT 56

When Leeds reached the European Cup final for the first time, they were undone by poor refereeing decisions just as they had been in the Cup Winners Cup final two years earlier.

United had an aggregate 5-3 win over Swiss side FC Zurich in the first round, losing 2-1 away after a 4-1 home victory. They then had comfortable victories against Hungarians Ujpest Dozsa and Belgian side Anderlecht, winning all four games, to reach the semi-finals.

Against Barcelona at Elland Road United won 2-1 then held out to draw 1-1 in the Nou Camp despite having Gordon McQueen sent off.

In the final against Bayern Munich in Paris, United were the better side for much of the game despite losing Terry Yorath to injury. United had two penalty appeals turned down and in the 66th minute Peter Lorimer had a legitimate looking goal disallowed for offside.

Five minutes after Lorimer's goal was ruled out Bayern took the lead though Roth. Muller then added another with nine minutes remaining to secure a second successive European Cup for the Germans.

FACT 57

1976
'BITES YER LEGS' LEAVES

Norman Hunter, one of the toughest tacklers that football has ever seen, left Leeds in 1976 after fourteen years at the club.

Hunter gave up an electrical apprenticeship to join United in 1962 when he was aged fifteen. He went on to form an effective partnership at the back with Jack Charlton that lasted a decade as United rose from Division Two to become one of the best clubs in Europe.

He developed a reputation for firm but fair tackling and his nickname came about after a banner was held up by fans prior to the 1972 FA Cup final that read 'Norman Bites Yer Legs.' He was well thought of by his fellow players, winning the Professional Footballers Association player of the year award in 1973-74.

After 540 appearances for United, Hunter joined Bristol City on 28th October 1976, the day before his 32nd birthday. He went on to play for and manage Barnsley then Rotherham, and had a brief spell with United as caretaker manager in 1988.

Although not directly involved in the game since leaving a coaching role at Bradford City in 1990, Hunter has worked as a summariser for radio in Yorkshire and been on the after dinner circuit. His autobiography, published in 2004, was entitled *Biting Talk*.

FACT 58

1978
JOCK STEIN'S
44 DAYS

Four years after Brian Clough lasted just 44 days as manager, Jock Stein was in the post for exactly the same length of time. However his departure was much more amicable than Clough's.

Stein had won ten Scottish League Championships and a European Cup with Celtic, but was replaced by Billy McNeill after a disappointing 1977-78 season. Although Celtic offered Stein a marketing position, he left as he wanted to stay in management.

After Jimmy Armfield was dismissed as the board felt he could take United no further, Stein was appointed two days after the start of the season. However results were mixed and it soon became apparent that Stein's heart remained in Scotland, where his family had continued to reside.

When the managerial vacancy for the Scottish national side came available, Stein couldn't be persuaded to stay at Elland Road. He hadn't signed a contract and was allowed to walk away with no hard feelings after 44 days in charge.

Stein was replaced by Jimmy Adamson, who guided United to a fifth place finish, their joint highest since winning the title in 1974.

1979
JOHN LUKIC

FACT 59

Goalkeeper John Lukic made his league debut on 13th October 1979, the first of 146 consecutive league appearances for Leeds United.

Aged just eighteen, Lukic first appeared for United in a European game against Valletta on 3rd October. Ten days later he replaced David Harvey in a league game at Brighton. This was the start of a remarkable run of consecutive league games that only ended on 12th March 1983, when he was dropped for a game against Newcastle after asking for a transfer.

Lukic was desperate for full England honours and didn't believe that continuing to play in Division Two

would be beneficial to him. He was signed by Arsenal where he remained for seven years, returning to Leeds in 1990 when he became the club's first £1 million signing.

In his second spell at Elland Road Lukic won the Division One title and played a total of 265 times. When Nigel Martyn was signed in the summer of 1996 Lukic rejoined Arsenal where he was understudy to David Seaman. A testimonial game was held in his honour at Elland Road, where he played a half for the Gunners and a half for United.

FACT 60

1980
ALLAN CLARKE
TAKES OVER

After Jimmy Adamson was sacked as manager, Leeds turned to a former player to get things back on track.

Adamson was sacked in September 1980 with United second to bottom of the table after six games. The club turned to former striker Allan Clarke, who had won promotion from Division Four with Barnsley and looked capable of taking them further up the leagues.

Clarke had been nicknamed 'Sniffer' in his playing days because of his ability to sniff out goals. He had scored 151 goals in 351 appearances for United, including the winning goal in the 1972 FA Cup final. He also won a Division One title and the Fairs Cup.

On taking over at Elland Road Clarke promised a trophy within three years. He immediately set about making United difficult to beat, tightening up the defence. It worked and they climbed the table to finish ninth. However there was very little entertainment as fans were subject to seven 0-0 draws and ten 1-0 wins.

There were also some times when the defence had a bad off day, such as when United were hammered 5-0 by Arsenal at Elland Road. Clarke had steadied things though and if there could be an injection of firepower, there was every reason to be optimistic for 1981-82.

FACT 61

1982 RELEGATION

Despite the promise shown the previous season and a record signing, 1981-82 was a disastrous season for Leeds United and ended in relegation.

In the summer of 1981 United paid West Bromwich Albion a club record £930,000 for Peter Barnes. The winger was expected to score and create goals for a side that had a mean defence which was further strengthened by the signing of Frank Gray.

Things got off to the worst possible start when United were hammered 5-1 at newly promoted Swansea. They won just one of their first ten games and Allan Clarke turned to the transfer market again, bringing in Kenny Burns to bolster the defence.

United rallied briefly in December but a 1-0 defeat at Arsenal on 23rd January started off a run of only one win from twelve. In March striker Frank Worthington arrived from Birmingham in an exchange deal for Byron Stevenson. Although he weighed in with goals, United were still leaking them at the back.

In the last home game of the season United beat Brighton 2-0, meaning a draw in their final fixture, away to West Bromwich Albion, would keep them up. However they lost 2-0 and were back in Division Two for the first time since 1964.

1985
LIVE TELEVISION CAMERAS

FACT 62

Leeds' first live televised match (apart from cup finals) was against Everton in the third round of the FA Cup on 4th January 1985.

United were drawn at home to the cup holders and current league leaders. The BBC chose this as their featured game in only the second season that the earlier rounds of the FA Cup were televised live.

The crowd was a lower than would be expected 21,211 and United received a £15,000 fee to offset the loss of gate income. They were the better team in the first half hour with visiting keeper Neville Southall making good saves from a John Sheridan free kick and a Peter Lorimer shot.

In the 39th minute Everton were awarded a penalty when the ball bounced up in the area and hit Andy Linighan's hand. It appeared accidental but the linesman flagged, the referee pointed to the spot and Graeme Sharp converted.

As much as United tried after the break, they were missing the injured Andy Ritchie in attack. Midway through the half Kevin Sheedy scored from close range for Everton and there was no way back now.

However United hadn't disgraced themselves against a side that finished the season as Football League champions, European Cup Winners Cup winners and FA Cup semi-finalists.

1985
NICE GUY EDDIE LEAVES

FACT 63

When Eddie Gray left the club in October 1985, it was not an easy decision for the board, nor was it popular amongst fans.

A skilful winger, Gray made his debut for United in 1966 aged just seventeen. However his playing career was blighted by injury and he missed much of the 1973-74 title winning season.

After United were relegated in 1982, Gray was appointed player-manager. With finances tight, he relied on bargain buys and youth, but United's free flowing football was good to watch and they had two successive top half finishes.

For the 1984-85 season Gray retired from playing and United won their opening four games. However they couldn't maintain this consistency and eventually finished seventh, five points off third place.

Prior to 1985-86 Ian Snodin arrived from Doncaster for £250,000 but United failed to win any of their first five games. There was a slight improvement but a 3-1 defeat at Huddersfield on 5th October left them in fourteenth.

Six days later Gray left the club by mutual consent after a 6-2 board vote went against him. It wasn't a popular decision amongst fans who called for the resignation of chairman Leslie Silver during the following day's 1-0 home win over Middlesbrough. Gray later returned to United as youth coach and was appointed manager again in 2003.

1985
PETER LORIMER'S
LAST GOAL

FACT 64

Leeds' record goalscorer is Peter Lorimer, who scored his last goal for the club twenty years after his first one.

Lorimer made his debut against Southampton in December 1962 at the age of just fifteen years and 289 days, but he did not become a first choice player until 1965-66.

He finished that season as the United's leading scorer with nineteen league goals from 34 appearances.

A right winger who could also play just off the main striker, Lorimer has a

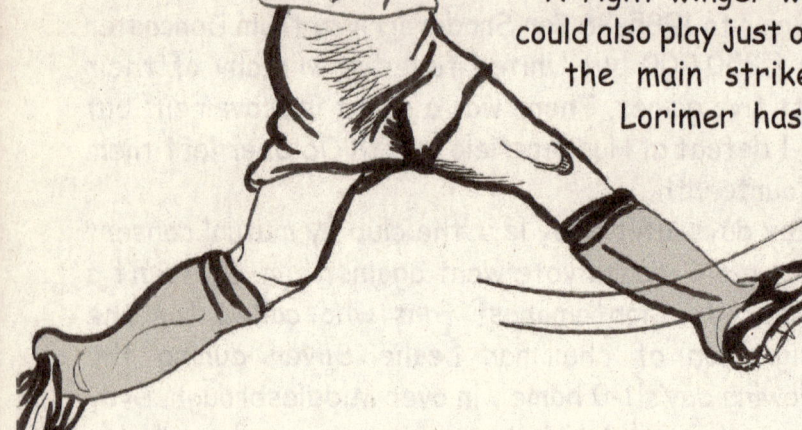

thunderous shot which was once measured at more than 75 miles per hour. In 1967-68 when United won two trophies he scored thirty goals in all competitions and was a league title winner in 1969 and 1974.

Lorimer left United in 1979 and joined York City then had spells in Canada with Toronto Blizzard and Vancouver Whitecaps. He made a surprise return to Elland Road during the 1983-84 season at the age of 37.

During Lorimer's second spell with United he broke John Charles's scoring record. However after Eddie Gray was sacked as manager, he didn't feature in replacement Billy Bremner's plans. The last of Lorimer's 238 goals for United came on 14th October 1985, when he scored a penalty in a 6-1 defeat at Manchester City in the short lived Football League Full Members Cup.

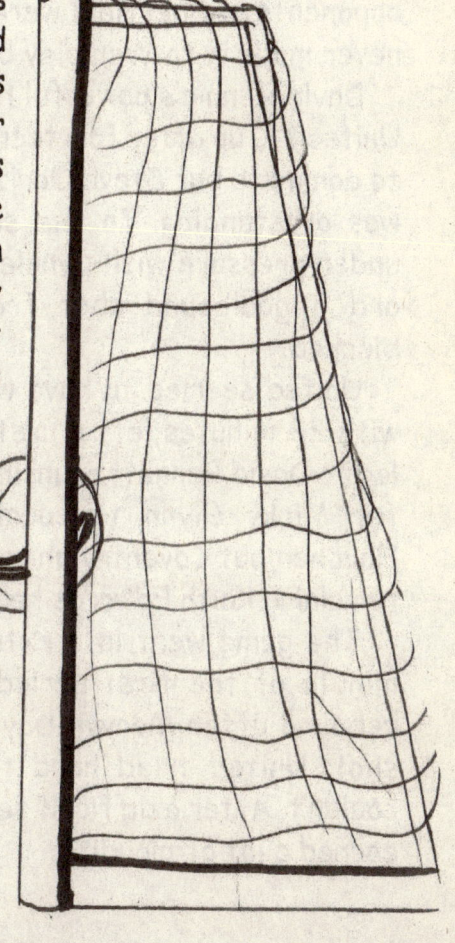

FACT 65
1987 FA CUP SEMI-FINAL HEARTACHE

Leeds played in one of the best ever FA Cup semi-finals in 1987 but ended up on the losing side after extra time.

United beat Telford, Swindon, QPR and Wigan to reach their first major semi-final in ten years. Their opponents in Sheffield were Coventry City, who had never made it to Wembley before.

David Rennie's powerful header from a corner put United 1-0 up after fourteen minutes. They continued to dominate but Steve Ogrizovic in the Coventry goal was outstanding. In the second half, Leeds were under pressure with Cyrille Regis proving a handful and a goalbound shot from Keith Houchen was blocked.

United seemed to have weathered the storm but with 22 minutes left a mistake by Brendan Ormsby led to David Bennett pouncing on the ball and crossing for Micky Glynn to equalise. Ten minutes later Houchen put Coventry ahead but with seven minutes remaining Keith Edwards headed in United's equaliser.

The game went into extra time and in the ninth minute of the first period Bennett seized on the rebound after Mervyn Day had stopped a Houchen shot. United tried hard to find an equaliser but couldn't. After a difficult few years though, they had earned a lot of plaudits.

1987
FIRST PLAYOFF FINAL

FACT 66

Leeds were involved in the first Football League playoffs in 1986-87 but they were denied promotion after being beaten in the final.

After finishing fourth in Division Two, United faced Oldham in a two legged playoff, winning the first leg 1-0 at Elland Road. Although they were beaten 2-1 away from home, they progressed on the away goals rule.

The final was a two legged affair against Charlton, who had occupied the last relegation place in Division One. United lost 1-0 away from home, then won the return leg by the same score. However there were no penalties and a third game was necessary at a neutral ground.

The vast majority of the 18,000 crowd at St Andrews in Birmingham on 29th May 1987 were supporting United. With the score 0-0 after ninety minutes the game went into extra time and John Sheridan's free kick gave United the lead in the first period.

With seven minutes remaining United looked set to be returning to the top flight but two goals from Peter Shirtliff enabled Charlton to preserve their status. It was heartbreaking for United but it had been a season of progress and manager Billy Bremner's contract was extended.

FACT 67
1988
BILLY BREMNER LEAVES

After failing to build on the promise shown in 1986-87, Billy Bremner left Leeds United in September 1988.

After Bremner was given a three year contract extension, United spent big in the summer of 1987. They signed Glynn Snodin, Gary Williams and Bobby Davison from Division One clubs and started the season as promotion favourites.

United then went on to have a disappointing start, winning just three out of the opening fifteen games and dangerously close to the relegation zone. They rallied in December with five straight wins but never looked like challenging for promotion, eventually finishing seventh.

There was another poor start to 1988-89 when just one win from the first six matches saw United only three points above the bottom club. Drastic action was taken and Bremner was sacked, to be replaced soon afterwards by Howard Wilkinson.

Bremner returned to manage Doncaster, where he had been between 1978 and 1985. Things didn't go well there and he resigned in November 1991, going onto the after dinner speaking circuit.

In December 1997 Bremner died of a heart attack at the age of just 55. A statue of him now stands at Elland Road and in 2006 he was voted as United's greatest player of all time.

FACT 68

1988
SERGEANT WILKO

When Leeds appointed Howard Wilkinson to replace Billy Bremner, he immediately set about removing all reminders of past glories.

When Wilkinson was appointed United were second bottom in the table with six points from nine games. It meant that persuading Wilkinson to leave Sheffield Wednesday, who were in the top half of Division One, was a big coup for the club.

Wilkinson was quick to impose his authority at Elland Road, ordering all photos from the Revie era to be taken down. He also made changes to the backroom staff, replacing Norman Hunter with his former Wednesday coach Mick Hennigan.

United soon began getting results under Wilkinson, who dipped into the transfer market to bring striker Carl Shutt to Elland road for £50,000 from Bristol City. Shutt had played Wilkinson at Wednesday and instantly repaid this renewed faith, scoring a hat-trick in a 3-0 home win over Bournemouth on his debut.

Under Wilkinson United soon started climbing the table and in March 1989 he persuaded Scottish international midfielder Gordon Strachan to drop down a division, paying Manchester United £300,000 for him. United finished the season in tenth, which was a respectable placing given the terrible start they had.

FACT 69

1990
BACK IN
DIVISION ONE

Leeds were promoted in 1989-90 to end their eight year exile from the top flight.

The season didn't get off to an encouraging start, losing 5-2 at Newcastle. However a fifteen game unbeaten run took them into the top two and they stayed their all season.

A dip in form during March and April meant the promotion race went right down to the last day. A win at Bournemouth would take United up as champions, but anything less and they could be in the playoffs.

In an extra twist, Bournemouth needed a win to avoid relegation while Newcastle, who could overhaul United, were playing at Middlesbrough. They themselves needed a win to stay up at Bournemouth's expense.

5,000 United fans travelled to the game at Bournemouth, with many more watching on CCTV in venues across Leeds. At half-time Middlesbrough were comfortably beating Newcastle so a point would be enough. Then four minutes after the restart Chris Kamara crossed and Lee Chapman headed home to send the travelling fans wild.

Bournemouth knew they were down and the rest of the game was played out in a carnival atmosphere created by the United fans. There were joyous scenes at the end and many fans went to the beach to celebrate, taking advantage of the ninety degree temperatures.

FACT 70

1992
DIVISION ONE
CHAMPIONS

Leeds were Division One champions in 1991-92 in the last season before the formation of the Premier League.

Prior to the start of the season Howard Wilkinson spent big, bringing in both Tony Dorigo and Rod Wallace for over a million pounds. United got off to a great start and were unbeaten in their first ten games. When they did lose at Crystal Palace, it didn't upset their momentum and they went on another unbeaten run, meaning that by the beginning of February they had lost just once in 27 games.

That month Eric Cantona arrived from Nimes to bring some extra creativity to the attack, but United suffered surprising defeats at Oldham and QPR. On 4th April a 4-0 loss at Manchester City was potentially damaging, but Manchester United couldn't capitalise and won just one of their next five games.

On 26th April United beat Sheffield United 3-2 at Bramall Lane in a lunchtime kick off. Later that afternoon, Liverpool beat Manchester United 2-0 meaning that the championship trophy was returning to Yorkshire after eighteen years.

The following Saturday there were jubilant scenes at Elland Road as the trophy was presented to captain Gordon Strachan before the game with Norwich. The match itself was not a classic, but United won 1-0 to complete an unbeaten home campaign.

1992
EUROPEAN REPRIEVE

FACT 71

Leeds thought they and been eliminated from the Champions League at the first hurdle in 1992-93, only to find their opponents had fielded an ineligible player.

United were drawn against German champions Stuttgart but were soundly beaten 3-0 away from home in the first leg. At Elland Road, Gary Speed gave United a first half lead before Buck equalised. Gary McAllister made it 2-1 before half-time but Leeds still needed three more goals to go through.

In the second half United threw everything they could at the German side, with goals from Eric Cantona and David Batty levelling the tie. Stuttgart still had the crucial away goal though and held on for the narrowest of victories.

Afterwards though it became apparent that Stuttgart had made a substitution that meant they had four foreign players on the pitch when UEFA rules only allowed three. UEFA then ordered both teams to play a one off game at Barcelona's Nou Camp stadium to determine who would go through.

There were just 7,000 fans present inside a stadium that held over 100,000. Goals from Carl Shutt and Gordon Strachan gave United a 2-1 win and took them through. However they couldn't carry their luck any further and were eliminated by Rangers in the next round.

FACT 72

1993
NO AWAY WINS
ALL SEASON

After the euphoria of winning the league, Leeds had a very disappointing campaign in 1992-93, failing to win away from home all season.

There were high hopes after United won the Charity Shield, beating Liverpool 4-3 at Wembley in a thrilling game in which Eric Cantona scored a hat-trick. However they failed to carry that forward when the season proper started.

At Elland Road Leeds were almost unbeatable. There were impressive wins over Tottenham (5-0) and Blackburn (5-2) and they lost only once, a 4-1 defeat by Nottingham Forest.

Away from home though, a 4-1 loss at Middlesbrough in the third game of the season was an indication of what was to come.

There were 4-0 defeats at both Manchester City and Tottenham, while United also conceded four goals at both Ipswich and Norwich, losing 4-2 each time.

Over the course of the season, Leeds had played 21 away games in the league and drew seven, losing fourteen. Although United never really looked like going down, they did end up finishing just two points above the relegation zone after winning none of the last six games.

FACT 73

1994
THE EAST STAND

In 1993 the conversion of Elland Road into an all seater stadium gathered pace as the largest cantilever stand in the world opened.

With government legislation requiring top flight stadia to become all seater, Leeds had to act otherwise the capacity of Elland Road would have fallen below 30,000. Various options were considered but to minimise disruption and cost the club opted to go for one large two tier stand.

Soon after United had been confirmed as champions in May 1992, the Lowfield Roads stand was knocked down. The steel framework then went up and dwarfed the other three sides of the ground. In February 1993 the 9,000 seat lower tier began to open in stages.

The upper tier, which had 6,000 seats, was in use from August 1993 while work continued on executive boxes and concourses. The whole project finished in January 1994 at a cost of £5.5 million, just a quarter of what it would have been to expand the Kop and West Stand. The development allowed Elland Road to host three matches during Euro 96.

The cantilever roof span of 51 metres surpassed the previous record of 48 metres at the Husky Stadium in Seattle. This was overtaken a few years later when Manchester United erected a new stand at Old Trafford.

FACT 74

1994
PHIL MASINGA & LUCAS RADEBE

Leeds signed two South Africans in the summer of 1994 but they went on to have contrasting fortunes with the club.

Phil Masinga and Lucas Radebe each cost £250,000 and arrived from Mamelodi Sundowns and Kaizer Chiefs respectively.

Masinga was a first choice striker with the South African national side but couldn't command a regular place at Elland Road. He showed individual skill but sometimes struggled to fit into the team pattern.

Masinga's best moment came when he scored a hat-trick against Walsall in an FA Cup tie in January 1995. He left for Swiss side St Gallen in 1996 as he hadn't played enough games to renew his work permit, but his professionalism and attitude could never be questioned.

Defender Radebe, on the other hand, enjoyed a much more successful United career and as captain led the side into the Champions League. A good reader of the game, he won a FIFA fair play award in 2000 and attracted interest from European giants AC Milan.

A serious knee injury meant Radebe missed the whole of 2001-2 and he struggled to regain his previous form on his return. He retired in 2005, having made a total of 256 appearances for United. He returned to his native South Africa, where he has coached the national side.

FACT 75

1995
TOMAS BROLIN

Arguably Leeds' biggest transfer flop was Tomas Brolin, who failed to live up to his superstar reputation when he signed in November 1995.

Brolin had been the star player for the Sweden side that finished third in the 1994 World Cup. The attacking midfielder had enjoyed a prosperous spell in Italy with Parma, winning the European Cup Winners Cup with them.

After joining United for £4.5 million Brolin scored four goals in his first eight games, but then expressed concern at how much defending he had to do in a 5-0 defeat at Liverpool. After being benched for the League Cup final against Aston Villa, he then suggested his future may lay elsewhere.

Having failed to secure a move in the summer, Brolin failed to arrive for pre-season training and was fined by Howard Wilkinson. He was then loaned to Swiss side FC Zurich for to months before agreeing another loan move back at Parma.

When Parma didn't make his loan permanent Brolin was back at United and put in the reserves. His contract was eventually terminated at the end of October 1997 and he joined Crystal Palace, where he failed to score in fifteen appearances. In 2007 *The Times* featured what it believed was the top fifty worst Premier League transfers, with Brolin listed at number four.

FACT 76
1996 LEAGUE CUP FINAL DISAPPOINTMENT

Leeds reached a Wembley final for the first time in 23 years in 1995-96, but were outplayed by Aston Villa.

On their way to Wembley United played only one other Premiership side, beating champions Blackburn in the fourth round. The semi-final was a comfortable 5-1 aggregate win over Birmingham, setting up a final date with their city rivals Villa.

A great strike from Savo Milosevic after a mistake by Gary Speed gave Villa a half-time lead and United looked tired going into the break. Brian Deane was brought on to give some more physical presence in attack but ten minutes after the restart Ian Taylor scored.

United were tired and never looked like getting back into the game, the introduction of Tomas Brolin doing nothing to change things. With two minutes remaining Dwight Yorke completed United's misery when he made it 3-0.

It was a bitterly disappointing day for United, with some fans turning on manager Howard Wilkinson. One bright spot was the performance of eighteen year old Andy Gray, who showed flashes of brilliance on the wing reminiscent of his uncle Eddie.

FACT 77

1997
GEORGE GRAHAM'S
BORE DRAW SPECIALISTS

George Graham, who had won two league titles with Arsenal, took over at Leeds for the 1996-97 season but he failed to repeat his success at Elland Road.

Graham's championship sides of 1989 and 1991 had been famous for their tight defences, with '1-0 to the Arsenal' becoming a famous terrace chant amongst their fans. He applied the same solid defensive principles with United, but couldn't get goals at the other end either.

The season began with a 3-3 draw at Derby, but after that the goals dried up at both ends of the pitch. Of 38 games played, nine ended up in 0-0 draws and a further nine were either 1-0 wins or defeats.

Brian Deane was the club's leading scorer in the league with just five goals. Veteran striker Ian Rush arrived from Liverpool but he was way past his best and scored just three goals in 34 appearances.

United finished the season in eleventh place with 46 points, just six points off the relegation zone. They had scored just 28 goals, the worst total in the Premier League, but their goals against tally of 38 meant their defence was meaner than champions Manchester United.

1998
PLANE CRASH DRAMA

FACT 78

Leeds' players were extremely lucky on 30th March 1998 when their plane caught fire shortly after takeoff and crash landed.

Following a 3-0 defeat at West Ham United, the team's HS-748 turboprop plane took off from Stansted Airport shortly after midnight. At 150 feet an engine exploded and the pilot aborted the flight. The plane crash landed and overshot the runway with the nose wheel collapsing.

After quickly evacuating, the party of eighteen were taken to a medical centre to be checked over and miraculously there were no major injuries. Assistant manager David O'Leary injured his shoulder whilst forcing open the door and described the landing as like a roller coaster.

Pilot John Hackett was praised for his bravery, as he had just a few seconds to make a decision that ultimately saved the lives of all on board. Chairman Peter Ridsdale later revealed that Hackett told him the plane would have caught fire within thirty seconds if he had remained in the air.

The team eventually arrived back in Leeds at 7.30am the next morning after continuing their journey by coach.

FACT 79

2000 TRAGEDY IN ISTANBUL

Leeds' run to the semi-final of the UEFA Cup in 1999-00 was marred by the deaths of two fans who were attacked prior to the away leg against Galatasaray.

United disposed of Partizan Belgrade, Lokomotiv Moscow, Spartak Moscow, Roma and Slavia Prague to reach the last four, where they were drawn with Turkish side Galatasaray.

On the eve of first leg in Istanbul two United fans, Christopher Loftus and Kevin Speight, were stabbed in one of the city's squares and died from their injuries. UEFA refused to postpone the game and there was not even a minutes silence beforehand. In an intimidating atmosphere United lost 2-0, but the result by then was irrelevant.

Galatasaray then asked for the second leg to be played at a neutral venue for their own safety. In the end the game went ahead at Elland Road, with away fans being banned from attending. Eirik Bakke scored twice from the penalty spot in a 2-2 draw meaning United were out of the competition.

The tragic events had an impact on the rest of the season but United were able to hold on to third place and Champions League qualification for the first time.

FACT 80

2000
MARK VIDUKA'S FOUR GOALS

On 4th November 2000 Australian striker Mark Viduka spearheaded a great comeback against Liverpool, becoming the first Leeds United player to score four goals in a game for 29 years.

United had a number of players missing through injury and hadn't won in five games, so when Liverpool led 2-0 after twenty minutes at Elland Road things didn't look good. Viduka pulled one back in the 25th

minute and then got the equaliser two minutes into the second half.

Soon after the hour mark Liverpool went 3-2 ahead but United refused to give in. In the 73rd minute Viduka scored with a brilliant drive after a turn that completely wrong footed the Reds' defence. Three minutes later as opposition defenders appealed for offside Viduka lofted the ball over Sander Westerveld in the Reds' goal to put Leeds ahead for the first time.

Despite frantic efforts by Liverpool to secure an equaliser, Leeds held on for victory. It had been a magnificent performance by Viduka and shown why United had paid Celtic £6 million for him in the summer.

As well as completing one of Elland Road's great comebacks, Viduka had become the first United player to score four goals in a game since Allan Clarke did so against Burnley in 1971.

FACT 81
2001 CHAMPIONS LEAGUE SEMI-FINALISTS

Leeds' first and only appearance to date in the Champions League was a remarkable one, ending with them losing in the semi-final.

United overcame 1860 Munich in a qualifier then were drawn in a tough group alongside Barcelona, AC Milan and Besiktas. Things started badly for United with a 4-0 defeat in Barcelona but they recovered to beat AC Milan 1-0 at Elland Road.

United hammered Besiktas 6-0 at home then drew 0-0 in Istanbul. They then led Barcelona 1-0 for much of the game at Elland Road, but the Catalans snatched an injury time equaliser to draw 1-1. However United's destiny remained in their own hands and they drew 1-1 against AC Milan in the San Siro to go through.

In the second group stage United were twice beaten by Real Madrid. However two wins over Anderlecht, and a win and draw against Lazio were enough to reach the last eight, where they overcame Deportivo La Coruna 3-2 on aggregate.

In the semi-final United faced another Spanish side, Valencia. In the first leg at Elland Road on 2nd May, both sides tried their hardest but couldn't find a goal. The following week United lost 3-0, ending their dream of glory in what had been a memorable campaign.

FACT 82

2002
DAVID O'LEARY LEAVES

Manager David O'Leary, who had succeeded George Graham in 1998 and taken Leeds to the brink of European glory, was sacked in the summer of 2002 and the club's fortune's have never been the same since.

During his four years as manager O'Leary never finished outside the top six and spent over £100 million to turn Leeds into a major force who played entertaining football. However the spending had been in part as a result of a huge loan taken out by owner Peter Ridsdale, who had gambled on being able to repay it by qualifying for the Champions League every year.

In 2001-02 United were top of the league on New Year's Day but eventually finished outside the Champions League qualification places. O'Leary had admitted himself that he needed to take United into the Champions League every year so in some ways his sacking should have been no surprise. However the fact he was replaced by Terry Venables, who had seemingly put business and media interests ahead of football management, was a cause for concern.

That summer United sold Rio Ferdinand and Robbie Keane for a combined £37 million, but spent less than a tenth of that to bring in Nick Barmby. The true extent of United's financial crisis was becoming apparent.

FACT 83

2003
AVOIDING RELEGATION

After four years challenging at the top of the table, Leeds only just escaped relegation in 2002-03.

United began by winning their first two games, but both were against newly promoted teams and they soon began dropping down the table.

Terry Venables was dismissed in March with eight games remaining and United threatened with relegation. He was replaced by Peter Reid, who was sacked earlier in the season by bottom club Sunderland. United continued to struggle and when they faced title challengers Arsenal at Highbury in their penultimate game, they were just three points clear of the relegation zone.

United didn't hold out much hope but after just five minutes, Harry Kewell opened the scoring with a tremendous half volley.

Although Thierry Henry equalised after half an hour Ian Harte restored United's lead four minutes after the break. Dennis Bergkamp levelled the scores again and when Henry hit the post, an Arsenal win seemed inevitable.

Nobody accounted for Mark Viduka however. With two minutes remaining the Australian took a pass from Dominic Matteo and scored with a brilliant curling shot to send United's fans wild. The victory had ended Arsenal's title hopes but more importantly for United, ensured they would be playing Premier League football for the following season.

2004
RELEGATION AND FIRESALE

FACT 84

Leeds couldn't repeat their relegation escape act in 2003-04 and went down to the Championship, leading to a firesale of players.

United lost eight of their first twelve games to leave them bottom of the table. A 6-1 defeat at Portsmouth led to the sacking of Peter Reid and Eddie Gray was appointed manager for the second time.

Gray's first game in charge was a 2-0 defeat to fellow strugglers Bolton but United then went five games unbeaten to climb out of the bottom three. This was followed by a run of six straight defeats and after that they rarely looked like staying up.

Relegation was confirmed with a 4-1 defeat at Bolton on 2nd May with two more games still to go. United finished the season in nineteenth place, ahead of bottom club Wolves only on goals scored.

In March 2004 the club had been taken over by a Yorkshire consortium, giving some financial stability for the short term. However there was a drastic need to cut costs and during the summer 25 players left the club. There seemed little prospect of an immediate return to the Premier League with United having to rely on loanees and youngsters for 2004-05.

2005
A REMARKABLE COMEBACK

FACT 85

One of Leeds' greatest comebacks came in a Championship game at Southampton on 19th November 2005, when they came from 3-0 down to win 4-3.

United had made an encouraging start to 2005-06 but by the time this fixture came around they were fourteen points off an automatic promotion place.

Southampton were the better side in the first half and after 27 minutes Marian Pahars headed in

from close range. Nigel Quashie added a second eight minutes later. Just before half-time Dan Harding handled in the area and Quashie scored the penalty.

At the break Southampton made three substitutions due to injury but United' boss Kevin Blackwell urged his players to get themselves out of the mess they created. However for 25 minutes Southampton remained the better side, only for United to be thrown a lifeline when Paul Butler headed one back in the 71st minute.

Eight minutes later a defensive mix-up allowed David Healy to cross and Robbie Blake scored from just outside the six yard box. With six minutes left, United were awarded a penalty for handball and David Healy converted for the equaliser.

Southampton were a complete shambles and a United winner looked inevitable. It came within two minutes when Liam Miller drove home a low shot from twelve yards to cue wild celebrations.

FACT 86

2006
PLAYOFF HEARTBREAK

Leeds made the Championship playoffs in 2005-06 but there was heartbreak as they were beaten in the final.

After flirting with relegation in 2004-05, it was hoped there would now be a season of consolidation after Ken Bates bought a stake in the club, helping to steady the finances. Inspired by manager Kevin Blackwell's shrewd tactics, United surprised themselves and were third at the end of February. However they had to settle for the playoffs after winning just one of their last ten games.

In the semi-final United drew 1-1 at home to Preston then won 2-0 at Deepdale in the second leg. The final against Watford was to be held at the Millennium Stadium in Cardiff, where United were roared on by 40,000 fans.

Watford were fast and physical and better suited to the wet conditions on a pitch that was cut up after hosting a rugby union match two days before. Jay Demerit headed them ahead from a corner in the 25th minute and shortly before the hour James Chambers made it 2-0. United's misery was completed six minutes time when Darius Henderson scored a penalty after a foul by Shaun Derry.

Blackwell admitted United had failed to perform but was encouraged by positive progress at the club. The following season though things went horribly wrong.

FACT 87

2007
THE SCHOOLBOY PLAYER

The only player to appear for Leeds whilst still at school was Tom Elliot in 2006-07.

Elliot came through the club's youth system and was still in Year 11 and preparing for his GCSEs when he broke into the first team squad after the new year. His first experience was as an unused substitute at Hull on 30th January, but he came off

the bench three days later at Norwich.

In the game United led 1-0 at half-time thanks to a goal from Jonny Howson. However in the second half Norwich came back to lead 2-1. Soon after United fell behind Elliot was given his chance, coming on for Kevin Nicholls but the result remained the same.

Although Elliot was United's first schoolboy player he was not the youngest. That honour remains with Peter Lorimer, who was fifteen when he made his debut in 1962, prior to the school leaving age being raised.

Elliot played twice more before the end of the season and was given a full time contract, but he failed to live up to his early promise. He played just once more for United in a League Cup tie and had loan spells with Macclesfield, Bury and Rotherham before joining Scottish side Hamilton in January 2011.

FACT 88
2007
RELEGATION AND ADMINISTRATION

A year after missing out on promotion to the Premier League in the playoff final, Leeds were relegated to the third tier for the first time at the end of 2006-07.

The season started with a win and a draw, but United lost five out of the next six games. Manager Kevin Blackwell was dismissed but it was a month before a permanent replacement was found. During this spell United lost four games in a row, conceding four or more goals in three of them.

United appointed Dennis Wise who took charge for the home game with Southend on 28th October 2006. United won 2-0 but it was a short honeymoon period for him as they lost the next two games.

From the time Wise took over, United were never out of the bottom three. They rallied briefly in March, going five games unbeaten but it was too little too late.

A 1-1 home draw with Ipswich on 28th April virtually sealed United's fate. To stabilise the finances, the club entered administration which immediately incurred a ten point penalty from the Football League and confirmed their relegation.

During the summer, United were docked a further fifteen points for failing to comply with the terms of their administration, meaning they faced an uphill struggle to get back up.

FACT 89

2007
WIPING OUT THE MINUS TALLY

Infuriated by the Football League's deduction of fifteen points, Leeds won seven games running at the start of 2007-08 to put them back on track.

The season began with a difficult trip to Tranmere, one of the teams expected to be in the frame for promotion. United deservedly trailed at half-time but came back out a different team and overturned the deficit to win 2-1. The fightback was well and truly on and the following Saturday Southend were hammered 4-1 at Elland Road.

Another difficult away game at Nottingham Forest ended in a 2-1 victory. They then beat Luton 1-0 before making it five wins in a row with a 2-0 win home win over Hartlepool. United were now the only team in the division with a 100% record, but were bottom of the table with zero points.

Further victories over Bristol Rovers, who were beaten 3-0 away from home, then Swansea, defeated 2-0 at Elland Road, meant United had won seven games at the start of the season for the first time since the Don Revie era. They were now in eighteenth place and out of the relegation zone.

The following week the run came to an end with a 1-1 draw at Gillingham, but United had clearly proved the doubters wrong.

FACT 90

2008
MCALLISTER'S PLAYOFF AGONY

When Dennis Wise left Leeds in January 2008 Gary McAllister took over and led them to the playoffs where he endured Wembley heartbreak.

By the beginning of the year United were third, just six points behind leaders Swansea. However Wise left to take a backroom position at Newcastle, with Gary McAllister taking over at Elland Road.

The former United captain had an indifferent start, but results soon improved and they finished fifth. United had qualified for the playoffs and would have gone up automatically if it weren't for the points deduction.

In the first leg of the semi-final, United trailed Carlisle 2-0 at Elland Road but five minutes into injury time Dougie Freedman hammered in a loose ball to give them some hope. In the second leg at Brunton Park Howson gave United the lead early on to level the tie. Then with extra time looming, Freedman flicked the ball on to Howson whose low shot crept into the net to complete the comeback.

At Wembley United faced Doncaster but were unable to match their quality and after falling behind early in the second half never looked like getting back into it. It had been a disappointing end, but there was comfort for United' fans in knowing their club had a future, unlike the uncertainty of twelve months earlier.

FACT 91

2008
A DEBUT GOAL
IN 25 SECONDS

Leeds' new signing Luciano Becchio wasted no time making an impact on his league debut, scoring after just 25 seconds.

Argentine striker Becchio signed from Spanish third tier side Merida that summer and made his first start at Chester in a League Cup tie. Jermaine Beckford was the star man in that game, scoring a first half hat-trick as United won 5-2.

Becchio was left out of the side for the next game, a 2-0 home defeat to Oldham. He was then selected for the trip to Yeovil on 23rd August, which was United's third league game of the season.

With just 25 seconds gone Rui Marques played a long ball into the box and there seemed little danger. However in one movement Becchio turned and hammered the ball into the corner of the net. Despite the promising start, United couldn't build on Becchio's early goal and a second half penalty earned Yeovil a draw.

Becchio had made enough of an impression though to retain his place for the next game against Crystal Palace in the League Cup. He went on to score fifteen league goals that season and stayed at the club until January 2013 when he moved to Norwich.

2010
FA CUP
GIANT KILLERS

FACT 92

Despite being in the third tier Leeds rolled back the years in 2010 when they knocked Premier League champions Manchester United out of the FA Cup.

United first needed to beat non-league Kettering to set up this third round tie. It was an opportunity to renew old rivalries but there was both excitement and apprehension amongst the United support.

Manager Simon Grayson said he wanted the players to enjoy the game and see where it took them, while Manchester United boss Sir Alex Ferguson played some mind games, talking up United and saying they would be in the Premier League in a few years.

Roared on by 9,000 fans, United absorbed the early pressure then in the nineteenth minute Jermaine Beckford latched on to a Johnny Howson lobbed pass and slid the ball past Tomas Kuszczak.

Despite having Wayne Rooney and Dmitar Berbatov up front, Manchester United couldn't break down the United defence. Michael Owen missed a great chance and United almost made it 2-0 when Robert Snodgrass smashed a free kick off the bar and Beckford fired wide.

It was United's first victory at Old Trafford since 1981 and confirmed Grayson's status as one of the best young managers in the game.

FACT 93

2010
BACK TO
THE CHAMPIONSHIP

United secured promotion from League One at the second attempt, but they made their fans sweat as they struggled to maintain their early season form.

After losing just one of their opening 23 league games, United had opened up an eleven point gap on third place, only to then win just four out of eighteen.

By the beginning of April, United had dropped out of the automatic promotion places. They then rallied and by the final day of the season knew that victory at home to Bristol Rovers would be enough to go up.

There were 38,000 inside Elland Road, but the atmosphere was tense as if United slipped up, four other sides had a chance to overhaul them. It was a physical battle and United were dealt a serious blow when Max Gradel was red carded for stamping.

Two minutes into the second half Rovers took the lead. With nothing left to lose, Simon Grayson gambled on a change and this paid off almost straight away when the oncoming player Jonny Howson equalised.

In the 63rd minute Jermaine Beckford made it 2-1 and it was a tense last half hour as United held on. There were joyous scenes at the end as fans invaded the pitch and celebrated with the players, putting years of disappointment behind them.

FACT 94

2011
BEST SUPPORT OUTSIDE OF PREMIER LEAGUE

Leeds gave a good account of themselves in their first season back in The Championship, when they were the best supported club outside the Premier League.

The season began with a home defeat to Derby but United drew their next game then won three in a row. Form was inconsistent in the autumn with some high scoring home defeats, including a crazy 6-4 loss to Preston.

On 30th October United won 4-1 at Scunthorpe, the start of a twelve game unbeaten run. This came to an end with a 2-1 defeat at Cardiff on 4th January, but United then went another seven games without defeat.

A 4-1 defeat of fellow playoff hopefuls Nottingham Forest at Elland Road on 2nd April meant United were fifth in the table, four points clear of seventh place. However they picked up just two points from their next five games to drop down to ninth.

In their penultimate game United won 1-0 at home against Burnley 1-0 to leave them with an outside chance of making the playoffs. On the final day of the season United beat newly crowned champions QPR 2-1 at Loftus Road, but they were denied a playoff place due to Forest's win at Crystal Palace.

It had been a credible return to the second tier for United though. For the first time since 1990-91 four players had scored ten goals or more and the average home attendance of 27,297 was the highest outside of the Premier League.

FACT 95

2011 TRIBUTE TO GARY SPEED

When former Leeds player Gary Speed committed suicide in 2011, the team and fans paid him the best possible tribute in their next game.

Speed joined United from school in 1988 and was a key player in the 1992 title winning side. After 300 games for them, in 1996 he joined Everton, the club he supported as a boy.

On Sunday 27th November 2011 the football world was stunned to hear that the 42 year old, now managing Wales, had committed suicide. Fans rushed to leave floral and other tributes at the Billy Bremner statue at Elland Road.

On the Tuesday night prior to United's game at Nottingham Forest a minutes applause from both sets of fans preceded the kick-off. United's fans sang Speed's name almost non stop, the loudest being in the eleventh minute, his shirt number. After dominating the opening stages, it was apt that Robert Snodgrass opened the scoring towards the end of that minute.

United remained on top and Johnny Howson scored from twenty yards just before half-time. Four minutes after the restart, Luciano Becchio headed a third and midway through the half Adam Clayton hammered home the fourth from close range.

The victory was an emotional one and a fitting tribute to Speed after a difficult few days.

FACT 96

2013
FANS GIVEN
BEER MONEY BY MANAGER

Leeds fans at a pre-season friendly were given some beer money by the manager after seeing their team win 3-0.

United were struggling when Brian McDermott took over from Neil Warnock in April 2013. Warnock, who had replaced Simon Grayson in February 2012, had a reputation as a promotion specialist but United were looking more likely to go down than up.

McDermott guided United to a comfortable thirteenth placed finish. United travelled to Slovenia in pre-season, beating a Select XI 3-0 in their first match. After the game McDermott went to salute United's travelling fans and passed one of them a 50 Euro note through the fence after they chanted for him to buy their drinks.

The donation was witnessed by a reporter from the *Yorkshire Evening Post* who was told by the manager that it was all he had with him and he wished he could have given more. Photographs appeared later on social media of fans enjoying their beer near the ground with the caption 'Thanks to Big Mc quality.'

United began the 2013-14 season steadily and were always in contention for the playoffs. However a five game losing streak in December and January saw them drop to twelfth and when Italian businessman Massimo Cellino took over the club McDermott's contract was terminated.

FACT 97

2014
OPPOSITION FAIL TO SHOW UP FOR FRIENDLY

Leeds' preparations for the 2014-15 season didn't all go to plan when their opposition failed to turn up for a friendly.

The squad headed to Italy in pre-season for a training camp and arranged two friendlies. The first of these was a 16-0 hammering of amateurs FC Gherdeina, the club's biggest ever friendly win.

United's next game was scheduled to be against Romanian top flight side Viitorul Constanta on 13th July. However the side owned by legendary Romanian international Gheorghe Hagi failed to show up, leaving officials at the stadium in Santa Christina wondering what to do.

Concern was first expressed an hour before kick-off, with a tweet attributed to new United head coach Dave Hockaday saying that the opposition weren't there, but his players were ready and officials were present.

To provide some entertainment for the 200 supporters who had travelled, Hockaday split the squad up into two and a United XI played a United XI. The game was played over three thirds of twenty minutes each, with the side playing in blue and gold beating the whites 3-1.

FACT 98 — 2014
FROM CARETAKER TO MANAGER

After three spells as caretaker manager, Neil Redfearn was finally given the job on a long term basis during the 2014-2015 season.

Redfearn joined United in 2009 as an academy coach and also took charge of the reserve team. When Simon Grayson was dismissed in February 2012, Redfearn took over for four games prior to the appointment of Neil Warnock.

Warnock was sacked in April 2013 and Redfearn stood in for one game before Brian McDermott came in. He kept Redfearn on as a first team coach, combining that with the role of reserves manager.

When McDermott left at the end of 2013-14 Redfearn stepped down from first team a duties to run the Academy. Dave Hockaday became manager but was in charge just seventy days. This meant another caretaker stint for Redfearn, who won three and drew one of the four games prior to Darko Milanic's recruitment.

Milanic lasted just 32 days as manager and at the beginning of November 2014 Redfearn was confirmed as having agreed a one year contract. He lifted the club from near the relegation zone to mid table, but was removed from the position at the end of the season. He initially returned to the Academy but resigned soon afterwards and became manager at Rotherham.

FACT 99

2015
UWE ROSLER

Neil Redfearn's replacement as manager was in charge for longer during the close season than the season proper.

German Uwe Rosler was appointed on 20th May 2015 and brought in seven new players prior to the start of the new season which began on 8th August. United drew their first four games before winning at Derby and drawing again, this time at home to Brentford.

United then lost four out of the next five games, the only win coming at Milton Keynes. The last of these games was a 2-1 home defeat to Brighton, their third defeat in a row at Elland Road. With United still looking for a home win, Rosler was sacked on 19th October with a record of two wins from eleven league games. They had also been knocked out of the League Cup at the first hurdle by Doncaster.

United were eighteenth in the table Rosler was replaced by former Rotherham manager Steve Evans, who led the club to another mid table finish. He was sacked at the end of the season, the sixth manager to be dismissed by Massimo Cellino in just two years.

FACT 100

2017
SEASON TICKET REFUND

When Leeds failed to make the playoffs in 2016-17 the club honoured a pledge to refund 25% of the cost of season tickets to fans who had pledged their support early.

In April 2016 the club announced that any supporter who bought a season ticket for the next campaign prior to 31st May would receive the 25% refund if United failed to make the top six. They even pledged to increase this to 50% if more than 15,000 fans bought season tickets but this target was not reached.

With Gary Monk installed as manager, United had an indifferent start winning just one out of the first six. Things really started to pick up in October though and eight wins from ten lifted them up to third.

On 18th March United beat Brighton 2-0 to remain in fourth, but four defeats in six games during April saw them drop out of the playoff places. Both the last two games were drawn meaning United faced at least another season outside the Premier League.

The club announced that the pledge would be honoured and advised eligible fans how to apply for the refund, which was estimated by some to have cost up to a million pounds to implement.

The 100 Facts Series

Arsenal, *Steve Horton*	978-1-908724-09-0
Aston Villa, *Steve Horton*	978-1-908724-92-2
Celtic, *Steve Horton*	978-1-908724-10-6
Chelsea, *Kristian Downer*	978-1-908724-11-3
Leeds, *Steve Horton*	978-1-908724-79-3
Liverpool, *Steve Horton*	978-1-908724-13-7
Manchester City, *Steve Horton*	978-1-908724-14-4
Manchester United, *Iain McCartney*	978-1-908724-15-1
Newcastle United, *Steve Horton*	978-1-908724-16-8
Norwich City, *Steve Horton*	978-1-908724-93-9
Rangers, *David Clayton*	978-1-908724-17-5
Tottenham Hostpur, *Steve Horton*	978-1-908724-18-2
West Ham, *Steve Horton*	978-1-908724-80-9